The Daily Telegraph
Quick Crossword Book
41

Also available in Pan Books

The Daily Telegraph Giant General Knowledge Crossword Book 1–9
The Daily Telegraph Pub Quiz Book
The Daily Telegraph Mind Gym
The Daily Telegraph Quick Crossword Book 6-52
The Daily Telegraph Cryptic Crossword Book 17–65
The Daily Telegraph Quick Holiday Crosswords 1–3
The Daily Telegraph Cryptic Holiday Crosswords 1–3
The Daily Telegraph Big Book of Cryptic Crosswords 1–17
The Daily Telegraph Big Book of Quick Crosswords 1–17
The Daily Telegraph Large Print Cryptic Crosswords 1–2
The Daily Telegraph Large Print Quick Crosswords 1–2
The Daily Telegraph Japanese Puzzle Compendium
The Daily Telegraph Book of Word Games
The Daily Telegraph How to Crack a Cryptic Crossword
The Daily Telegraph Sudoku 1-7
The Daily Telegraph Holiday Sudoku 1–3
The Daily Telegraph Bumper Christmas Sudoku
The Daily Telegraph Book of Codewords 1–5
The Sunday Telegraph Book of General Knowledge Crosswords 1– 6

and in Macmillan

The Daily Telegraph 80 Years of Cryptic Crosswords
A Display of Lights (9): The Lives and Puzzles of the *Telegraph's*
     Six Greatest Crossword Setters

and for more titles visit www.panmacmillan.com

The Daily Telegraph

Quick Crossword Book
41

Pan Books

in association with *The Daily Telegraph*

First published in 2005 by Pan Books

This edition first published 2018 by Pan Books
an imprint of Pan Macmillan, a division of Macmillan Publishers Limited
Pan Macmillan, 20 New Wharf Road, London N1 9RR
Basingstoke and Oxford
Associated companies throughout the world
www.panmacmillan.com

In association with *The Daily Telegraph*

ISBN 978-1-509-89390-4

Visit **www.panmacmillan.com** to read more about all our books and to buy
them. You will also find features, author interviews and news of any author
events, and you can sign up for e-newsletters so that you're always first to hear
about our new releases.

ACROSS

1 Bright as a —— (6)
4 Entire (5)
8 Sea-air (5)
9 Turned down (7)
10 Insinuate (7)
11 Soon; unnamed (4)
12 Embrace (3)
14 Eye-sore (4)
15 Repose (4)
18 Scots river (3)
21 Weapons (4)
23 Beatified (7)
25 Nuclide (anag.) (7)
26 —— -utan (5)
27 Argot (5)
28 Abutting building (4-2)

DOWN

1 Lady's garment (6)
2 Idea (7)
3 Astonished; fully aware (4-4)
4 Spouse (4)
5 —— Welles (films) (5)
6 Gin den (anag.) (6)
7 Verity (5)
13 Grisly (8)
16 Support (7)
17 Church of England's daily morning service (6)
19 Flowed out (5)
20 Slowly (music) (6)
22 Islamic holy city (5)
24 Step of ladder (4)

2

ACROSS

1 Yehudi —— (music) (7)
8 Language (6)
9 Employment (7)
11 Car chain (anag.) (8)
12 Once more (5)
14 Spring; source (4)
15 Two-humped camel (8)
17 Dearth (8)
18 eg Pooh (4)
20 Pa (5)
21 Exceptional person (4,4)
23 Beforehand (7)
24 Pamper (6)
25 Leaving a will (7)

DOWN

2 Come out (6)
3 Uncover (6)
4 Early Peruvian (4)
5 In proportion (3,4)
6 —— *Melody* (1955 hit) (9)
7 Trickery (9)
10 Ape Turner (anag.) (9)
12 Smitten with wonder (9)
13 Ancient Mariner bird (9)
16 Skin infection (7)
18 eg *Giselle* (6)
19 Arrival (6)
22 Lady (4)

ACROSS

1 Fabulous bird (3)
3 Vase (3)
5 Function (4)
7 Competing (5)
8 Harm (6)
10 Run boundingly (4)
11 Whale food (8)
13 Twine (6)
14 Weak (6)
17 Hopeful person (8)
19 Defect (4)
21 More reasonable (6)
22 Asian language (5)
23 Piece of earth (4)
24 Wood for bows (3)
25 Observe narrowly (3)

DOWN

1 Turn (10)
2 Sailing vessel (7)
3 Exhort (4)
4 Head (slang) (6)
5 Memory-jogger (8)
6 Of little weight (5)
9 Guarantee (10)
12 Thoroughly beaten (colloq.) (8)
15 Equilibrium (7)
16 Missing (6)
18 Fish using nets (5)
20 Exhibit (4)

4

ACROSS

1 Carried (5)
4 Separate (5)
10 Changed (7)
11 Let in (5)
12 Musical drama (5)
13 Enlarge (anag.) (7)
15 Pour (4)
17 Compare (5)
19 Bury (5)
22 Day of month (4)
25 Set free (7)
27 Thespian (5)
29 Pigs (5)
30 Unity (7)
31 Knife (5)
32 Read to learn (5)

DOWN

2 Route (anag.) (5)
3 Recount (7)
5 Seafood (5)
6 Regret (7)
7 Wooden shoe (5)
8 Aphorism (5)
9 Coral island (5)
14 Exude (4)
16 Finishes (4)
18 Animosity (3-4)
20 Closest (7)
21 Expunge (5)
23 Writer of fables (5)
24 Iron; newspapers (5)
26 In front (5)
28 Step (5)

ACROSS

1 Church service (4)
4 Eurasian republic (6)
7 Employ (3)
9 Axe (4)
10 Owned up to (8)
11 Male sheep (3)
12 Small lake (4)
13 Lookouts (8)
16 Resolve (13)
19 Frailty (8)
23 Speechless (4)
24 Faucet (3)
25 Foreigner (8)
26 Possesses (4)
27 Infirm (3)
28 Cosmetics (4-2)
29 Relaxation (4)

DOWN

2 Accomplishments (12)
3 Sovereign (7)
4 Crews (5)
5 A typeface (5)
6 Go in (5)
8 MTD envelopes (anag.) (12)
14 Goes out (5)
15 Afternoon meal (3)
17 Managed (3)
18 Larval frog (7)
20 Arboreal marsupial (5)
21 Bird of prey (5)
22 Undress (5)

6

ACROSS

1 Correct (6)
4 Male goose (6)
7 Teacher (9)
9 Young salmon (4)
10 Expectorate (4)
11 HM's favourite dog (5)
13 Eke out (6)
14 Inventor (6)
15 Spice (6)
17 Colombian capital (6)
19 Characteristic (5)
20 Manage (4)
22 Let down (4)
23 Transitory (9)
24 Save (6)
25 Imp (6)

DOWN

1 Indigent person (6)
2 Equal (4)
3 Logic (6)
4 Name of six kings (6)
5 Common sense (4)
6 Corrupt (6)
7 Original model (9)
8 Governed by bishops (9)
11 Heavenly body (5)
12 Simpleton (5)
15 Divine drink (6)
16 Graham —— , author (6)
17 Arm muscle (6)
18 Seduce (6)
21 Heroic poem (4)
22 Impartial, so-so (4)

ACROSS

1 Ruminants' food (5)
4 Ways to travel (6)
9 Distinguished (7)
10 Unite (anag.) (5)
11 Look for (4)
12 Hellenic (7)
13 —— to a 12 Urn (3)
14 Ballet skirt (4)
16 Bird's prison (4)
18 Chopper (3)
20 Rumpled (7)
21 Mountain-goat (4)
24 Annulled; unfastened (5)
25 Carry on (7)
26 Bear (6)
27 Locates (5)

DOWN

1 Rock musical (6)
2 —— *in Wonderland* (5)
3 Pace (4)
5 Richness (8)
6 Adding (up) (7)
7 Hanks (6)
8 Gates (anag.) (5)
13 Someone excluded (8)
15 Turned over (2-5)
17 Point the finger at (6)
18 Skilful (5)
19 *Old Testament* book (6)
22 Sheep's call (5)
23 Fling (4)

ACROSS

1 Scilly isle (6)
4 Dense (5)
8 Aka (5)
9 Bazaars (7)
10 Looking closely (7)
11 Eye sore (4)
12 Finish (3)
14 Deer (4)
15 Decree (4)
18 Knight's title (3)
21 Wicket crosspiece (4)
23 Ripe mud (anag.) (7)
25 So you allege! (4,3)
26 Small bay (5)
27 Apollo's birthplace (5)
28 More hideous (6)

DOWN

1 Hobos (6)
2 Obvious (7)
3 Moulds (8)
4 Novice (4)
5 Passive (5)
6 Mouth (slang) (6)
7 Mental picture (5)
13 Falling (8)
16 Rhine siren (7)
17 Bad Sue (anag.) (6)
19 Bowler's approach (3,2)
20 Newspaper chief (6)
22 Rustic poem (5)
24 Cricket extras (4)

ACROSS

1 Fights (7)
5 Eccentric (4)
7 English composer (5)
8 Pillar (6)
10 Portal (4)
11 Golden land (8)
13 Rotter (anag.) (6)
14 Leaseholder (6)
17 Long race (8)
19 Quieten (4)
21 Attack verbally (3,3)
22 Accomplishing (5)
23 Personality (4)
24 Decorated china (7)

DOWN

1 Tiny piece of a loaf (10)
2 Towing vessel (7)
3 Songbird (4)
4 Reaping-hook (6)
5 Moor near Inverness (8)
6 Burma (anag.) (5)
9 Danish capital (10)
12 To destroy irredeemably (5,3)
15 Scrutinised (7)
16 Kicked (6)
18 Bonn's river (5)
20 Cutting tool (4)

10

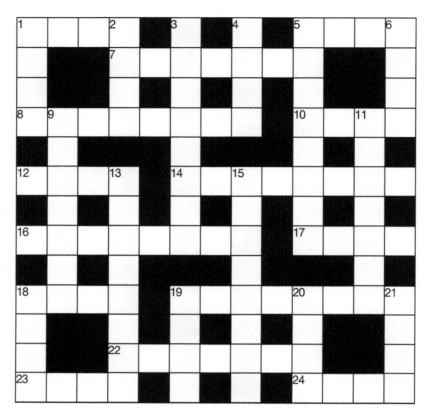

ACROSS

1 Dandy (4)
5 Fish; heather (4)
7 Spire (7)
8 Vision (8)
10 Classify; kind (4)
12 Moist (4)
14 Amaze (8)
16 An escort (anag.) (8)
17 Culinary herb (4)
18 Lazy (4)
19 Stated (8)
22 Sure (7)
23 Enormous (4)
24 Small branch (4)

DOWN

1 French cheese (4)
2 Utilises (4)
3 NCO (8)
4 See; place (4)
5 Needless (anag.) (8)
6 Present (4)
9 Longed (7)
11 Determination (7)
13 Make-believe (8)
15 Renegade (8)
18 Irritate (4)
19 Night (4)
20 Female relation (4)
21 Haul (4)

ACROSS

7 Jeered (6)
8 Authoritative statement (6)
10 Let go (7)
11 Wait in line (5)
12 Outbuilding (4)
13 Sorrow (5)
17 Alloy (5)
18 Prefix for thousand (4)
22 Requirements (5)
23 Cold dry wind (7)
24 Biochemical catalyst (6)
25 Medieval land-holder (6)

DOWN

1 Hold dear (7)
2 Liturgical book (7)
3 Muscular fellow (2-3)
4 Game on lawn (7)
5 Eightsome (5)
6 Gem (5)
9 Tedious (9)
14 Suppose (7)
15 eg Pepys (7)
16 Urbane (7)
19 Attach after conquest (5)
20 Grab (5)
21 Dissertation (5)

12

ACROSS

1 Strikes sharply (6)
4 Treatise (5)
8 Hydrophobic (5)
9 I lament (anag.) (7)
10 London borough (7)
11 Japanese pill-box (4)
12 The alphabet (3)
14 Leg joint (4)
15 Pawn (4)
18 Epoch (3)
21 Open-mouthed (4)
23 Legacy (7)
25 Trimmed (7)
26 —— Doolittle (5)
27 Cheek (5)
28 Agreement (6)

DOWN

1 Trill (6)
2 Egg-white (7)
3 Fish & rice dish (8)
4 Shroud (4)
5 Song of praise (5)
6 Allowance (6)
7 Russian country house (5)
13 Draughts (8)
16 Narrow crack (7)
17 Bird of prey (6)
19 Dwell; tolerate (5)
20 Royal house (6)
22 Willow (5)
24 Church recess (4)

ACROSS

1 South American capes (7)
5 Flier (5)
8 Ire (5)
9 Takes up again (7)
10 Gave evidence (9)
12 Nothing (3)
13 Funny play (6)
14 Equilibrium (6)
17 Unwell (3)
18 Old army musket (5,4)
20 Clothes fasteners (7)
21 Dodge (5)
23 Cattle estate (5)
24 All tire (anag.) (7)

DOWN

1 eg Flower (5)
2 Complain, worry (3)
3 Hastened (7)
4 Pulled muscle (6)
5 Sat for painter (5)
6 Glow (9)
7 Struggles (7)
11 Idiot (9)
13 Mountaineer (7)
15 Line touching curve (7)
16 I floss (anag.) (6)
18 Stall at fair (5)
19 Carapace (5)
22 Atmosphere (3)

14

ACROSS

1 Capital of Jordan (5)
4 Wild, untamed (5)
10 Adds herbs or spices (7)
11 Tudor king (5)
12 Austrian composer (5)
13 I'm a liar (anag.) (7)
15 Organs of hearing (4)
17 Novel Swiss girl (5)
19 Whiskey (5)
22 Got up (4)
25 Express dissent (7)
27 —— Woods (golf) (5)
29 Gold weight (5)
30 Obvious (7)
31 Dismay (5)
32 Hebridean isle (5)

DOWN

2 Fleshy (5)
3 Embellished (7)
5 Anaesthetic (5)
6 Yearbooks (7)
7 —— crow flies (2,3)
8 Hollywood award (5)
9 Bike (5)
14 Egyptian goddess (4)
16 Tunes (4)
18 Got ripe (anag.) (3-4)
20 Sells (7)
21 Particle (5)
23 Alternate (5)
24 Soup (5)
26 Special edition (5)
28 —— Garbo (5)

ACROSS

1 Vale (6)
7 Enunciation (7)
8 Undo clothing (8)
9 Upper room (5)
10 Dog-like animal (5)
11 Cab (4)
12 Freezing (5)
15 Pseudonym (5)
16 Broil (5)
19 Seaweed (4)
20 Adhere (5)
21 Excitable (5)
22 Greenhouse (8)
23 Collapse (7)
24 —— *Spirit* (Noel Coward) (6)

DOWN

1 Testifying (8)
2 Opera texts (8)
3 Supplementary (5)
4 Succeed (3)
5 Unmoving (6)
6 Balm (6)
7 Dogmatic (11)
9 Straight line (4)
13 About to happen (8)
14 Carved spout (8)
15 Friend (4)
17 Rushes (anag.) (6)
18 Prodigal (6)
20 Waterway (5)
22 Unusual (3)

16

ACROSS

1 Inscribe (5)
4 Sounded dejected (6)
9 Pasta dish (7)
10 Frequently (5)
11 Second-hand (4)
12 Detests (7)
13 Hard; place (3)
14 Beat (anag.) (4)
16 Roster (4)
18 Produce eggs (3)
20 Defeat (7)
21 People; run (4)
24 Denoting four (prefix) (5)
25 Military man (7)
26 Mock (6)
27 Discrimination (5)

DOWN

1 Marine mammal (6)
2 Publication (5)
3 Border (4)
5 Adroitly (anag.) (8)
6 Axe (7)
7 Ruler (6)
8 Traded (5)
13 Flag (8)
15 Smoked herring (7)
17 Asserted (6)
18 Minimum (5)
19 Ordain (6)
22 Zodiacal sign (5)
23 Boring; apartment (4)

ACROSS

1 Bird's mouth (4)
4 Husky (6)
7 Anger (3)
9 Norse god (4)
10 Woke up (8)
11 Leg (anag.) (3)
12 Lacking hair (4)
13 Guards (8)
16 Act of remembrance (13)
19 Comes before (8)
23 Mute (4)
24 Hat (3)
25 Of a lower standard (8)
26 Possesses (4)
27 Trouble (3)
28 Value highly (6)
29 Relaxation (4)

DOWN

2 Striving (12)
3 Realm (7)
4 Cures (5)
5 Anew (5)
6 Very steep (5)
8 Move Len's dept (anag.) (12)
14 Wear away (5)
15 Hot drink (3)
17 Female sheep (3)
18 Larval frog (7)
20 Board game (5)
21 Impel (5)
22 Go away! (5)

18

ACROSS

1 Stream (5)
4 Big cat (7)
8 Reclaim (anag.) (7)
9 Waterlily (5)
10 On high (5)
11 Rational (7)
13 Abound (4)
15 Chest (6)
17 Avoided (6)
20 Hebridean island (4)
22 Souvenir (7)
24 Automaton (5)
26 Heels; rolls (5)
27 Made redundant (4,3)
28 Exam marks (7)
29 eg The Ritz (5)

DOWN

1 Unrestrained (7)
2 Star sign (5)
3 Italian cheese (7)
4 Boy's voice (6)
5 USSR prison camp (5)
6 Lured (7)
7 Rope-making fibre (5)
12 Portent (4)
14 Go out (4)
16 Absorptive process (7)
18 Gloss finish (7)
19 Loyal and obedient (7)
21 Lots (6)
22 Back tooth (5)
23 Of the nose (5)
25 Promote (5)

ACROSS

1 Crepe (7)
5 Lift (5)
8 Subsequently (5)
9 Songs (7)
10 —— *Bells* (Mike Oldfield) (7)
11 Indo-European (5)
12 Native of Brittany (6)
14 Industrial action (6)
17 Squabbled (5)
19 Frying pan (7)
22 Henry ——, songwriter (7)
23 Illegal act (5)
24 On lad (anag.) (5)
25 Rude remarks (7)

DOWN

1 Ship's guide (5)
2 Ton bale (anag.) (7)
3 Fourth month (5)
4 Board ship (6)
5 Dependent (7)
6 Country (5)
7 Distinctive nature (7)
12 —— *of Alcatraz* (film) (7)
13 Police (slang) (3,4)
15 Animosity (3-4)
16 Birthplace of St Francis (6)
18 Decreased in size (5)
20 Peruvian natives (5)
21 Elms, pines etc (5)

20

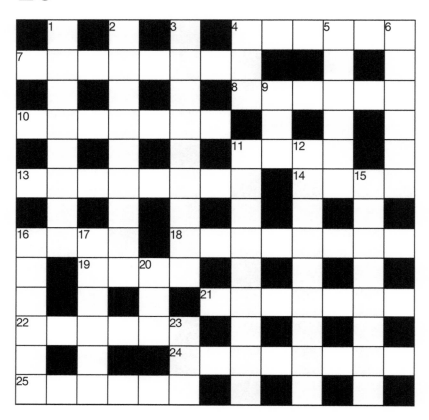

ACROSS

4 BBC nickname (6)
7 Plane (8)
8 Warning notice (6)
10 Staying power (7)
11 Depressed (4)
13 Lift vase (anag.) (8)
14 Beg (4)
16 Drug taker (4)
18 Handed over (8)
19 eg Hoy, Yell or Sark (4)
21 Ancient Persian god (7)
22 Greek capital (6)
24 Contrive (8)
25 Printing errors (6)

DOWN

1 Peril (8)
2 Turkish swords (9)
3 Flesh eater (9)
4 WW2 female service (3)
5 Fragile (6)
6 Funeral oration (6)
9 Ailing (3)
11 Lord Emsworth's castle
(P G Wodehouse) (9)
12 Advantage (5-4)
15 Save rage (anag.) (8)
16 Insecure (6)
17 One of two (6)
20 Sir —— Hutton (3)
23 eg Galilee (3)

ACROSS

1 Pouring forth (7)
5 1000 kilograms (5)
8 Gather together (5)
9 Observed (7)
10 Acquit (9)
12 View; prelacy (3)
13 Ten years (6)
14 Pester (6)
17 Poem (3)
18 Banal (9)
20 Drinkable (7)
21 Contempt (5)
23 Traded (5)
24 Wind about (7)

DOWN

1 Large marine mammal (5)
2 Pasture (3)
3 Stained (anag.) (7)
4 Cordial (6)
5 Name (5)
6 Essential (9)
7 Non-stop (7)
11 Other cars (anag.) (9)
13 Fell (7)
15 Loss of memory (7)
16 Yell (6)
18 Custom; riding dress (5)
19 Benefactor (5)
22 Strange (3)

22

ACROSS

1 Small inlet (5)
4 Radiators (7)
8 Employ (3)
9 Also (3)
10 Visualisation (5)
11 Timbre (5)
12 Betrothed (7)
15 If not (4)
17 State chair (6)
19 Relation (6)
22 Classify (4)
24 Largest (7)
26 Theme (5)
28 Pedestal (5)
30 Spike of corn (3)
31 Only just beat (3)
32 Resolves (7)
33 Tales (5)

DOWN

1 Tea cake (7)
2 Happening (5)
3 Galley (7)
4 Ungulates' feet (6)
5 Copying (5)
6 Aeon (3)
7 Pay out (5)
13 Approach (4)
14 Eviscerate (3)
16 Not as much (4)
18 Tease (3)
20 Totally (7)
21 Breaks out (7)
23 Different ones (6)
24 Established (5)
25 Terminated (5)
27 Written essay (5)
29 Part of circle (3)

ACROSS

1 Grain store (7)
5 Propagated (4)
7 Glorify (5)
8 Recondite (6)
10 Trim (4)
11 Waterproof strip (8)
13 Doglike (6)
14 Mendicant (6)
17 Green tea (anag.) (8)
19 Diesel oil (4)
21 Dawn goddess (6)
22 Bed-cover (5)
23 + (4)
24 Applied wrongly (7)

DOWN

1 Good heavens! (5,5)
2 Forsake (7)
3 *New Testament* book; laws (4)
4 Per annum (6)
5 Free of charge (8)
6 Boredom (5)
9 Made worse (10)
12 Notorious (8)
15 Leg-armour (7)
16 Mabel C (anag.) (6)
18 Peer (5)
20 Chances (4)

24

ACROSS

1 Chopper (3)
3 Ocean (3)
5 Hollow (4)
7 Romany (5)
8 Car storage (6)
10 Jacob's brother (*Old Testament*) (4)
11 Charged particle (8)
13 At glen (anag.) (6)
14 See 17
17 & 14 Board game (4,4,6)
19 African tribesman (4)
21 Character (6)
22 Consumer magazine (5)
23 50 per cent (4)
24 Light metal (3)
25 eg Helium (3)

DOWN

1 Increasing (10)
2 Expound (7)
3 States (4)
4 —— and Sutherland Highlanders (6)
5 Board member (8)
6 African country & river (5)
9 Considering that (8,2)
12 Suet pudding (4,4)
15 Sour gin (anag.) (7)
16 Purpose (6)
18 Former name of Lake Malawi (5)
20 Identical sibling (4)

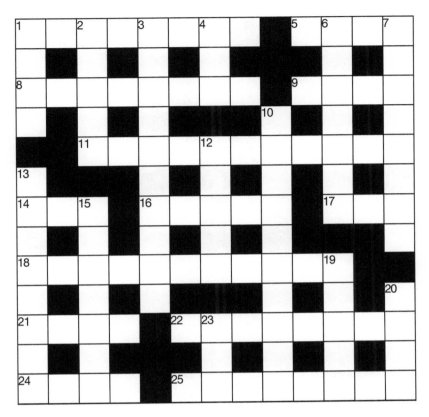

ACROSS

1 Content of a duet (3,5)
5 Gentle (4)
8 Make hostile (8)
9 Regimen (4)
11 Disfigurement (11)
14 Swiss mountain (3)
16 Sinned (5)
17 Allow (3)
18 Levels (11)
21 Slender (4)
22 Jawbone (8)
24 Expel (4)
25 Film about Elsa the lioness (4,4)

DOWN

1 eg Ash, oak (4)
2 Be rod (anag.) (5)
3 Ethylene glycol (10)
4 Draw (3)
6 Original (7)
7 Explode (8)
10 Female servant (10)
12 Broadcast again (5)
13 Cult of virility (8)
15 Lies (colloq.) (7)
19 Not drunk (5)
20 Brazilian footballer (4)
23 Fuss (3)

26

ACROSS

1 Indicator; missile (5)
4 Way of walking (4)
8 Navigational aid (7)
9 Formed with an arch (5)
10 Nonet (anag.) (5)
11 Perceive (7)
13 Small and dainty (6)
15 Floodgate (6)
17 Liquid lost (7)
20 Escort (5)
22 Bedtime drink (5)
23 Branch of mathematics (7)
24 Comic sketch (4)
25 Unstick (5)

DOWN

1 Royal racecourse (5)
2 Strong protest (12)
3 Set of shelves (7)
4 Zest (5)
5 Bone in middle ear (5)
6 Small case (9,3)
7 Header (anag.) (6)
12 Motor-coach (3)
13 Insurance contract (6)
14 Ovum (3)
16 Reclined (7)
18 Taken —— ; surprised (5)
19 Precise (5)
21 Kingdom (5)

ACROSS

1 Tying (8)
7 Culinary herb (5)
8 Aperitif (9)
9 Unused (3)
10 Simple (4)
11 Going by air (6)
13 Bookish egghead (6)
14 Drawer (anag.) (6)
17 Show; cover (6)
18 Finest (4)
20 Adapt; well (3)
22 Easter-egg (anag.) (9)
23 Stupid (5)
24 Slope (8)

DOWN

1 Rogue (5)
2 Confronted (7)
3 Small children (4)
4 Snuggle (6)
5 Mendacious (5)
6 Marine plant (7)
7 Coach; footwear (7)
12 Singers (anag.) (7)
13 Exemplary (7)
15 The mean (7)
16 Mendicant (6)
17 Pilfer (5)
19 Twitter (5)
21 Peruse (4)

28

ACROSS

1 American cafe (5)
4 Power (5)
10 By the sea (7)
11 Raffles (5)
12 Primp (5)
13 Understand (7)
15 Items of information (4)
17 Shift (5)
19 Chants (5)
22 Eager (4)
25 Navigational tool (7)
27 Pier (5)
29 Qualified carer (5)
30 Put in order (7)
31 Whispered comment (5)
32 Embellish (5)

DOWN

2 Effigy (5)
3 Stretches (7)
5 Asian country (5)
6 Being in front of (7)
7 Ambit (5)
8 Warning signal (5)
9 Willow (5)
14 Facility (4)
16 Requests (4)
18 Comments (7)
20 Hurt (7)
21 Part of play (5)
23 Attempt (5)
24 Set by (anag.) (5)
26 Rectify (5)
28 Singing voice (5)

ACROSS

1 Largest mammal (5)
4 French wine region (6)
9 Costers (anag.) (7)
10 Insignia (5)
11 —— Fitzgerald (jazz) (4)
12 Commanded (7)
13 Large cask (3)
14 Child's toy (2-2)
16 God of love (4)
18 Insane (3)
20 European country (7)
21 Six balls (4)
24 Cornish town (5)
25 Great ape (7)
26 Most senior in age (6)
27 —— and groans (5)

DOWN

1 Basketwork (6)
2 Spring month (5)
3 Smooth, level (4)
5 Set in (8)
6 Endure, experience (7)
7 Alters, corrects (6)
8 & 22 Football club (5,5)
13 Devious, circuitous (8)
15 Not dour (anag.) (7)
17 Large sickle (6)
18 Madonna's nickname (5)
19 Norfolk holiday area (6)
22 See 8
23 Birmingham's nickname (4)

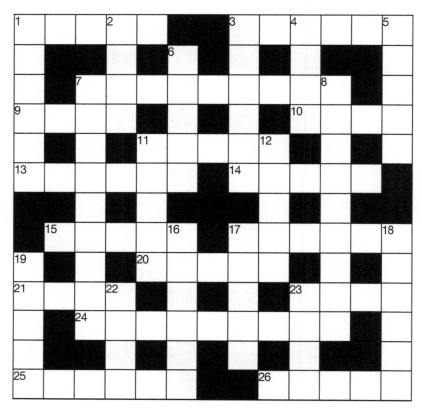

ACROSS

1 Donor (5)
3 Hoaxer (6)
7 Video/audio unit (9)
9 Hits (anag.) (4)
10 Seven days (4)
11 Entreaties (5)
13 Certainly (6)
14 Rover (5)
15 Nobleman (5)
17 Rude, base (6)
20 Prestige (5)
21 Superman's girl (4)
23 Vehemence (4)
24 Crushed noisily (9)
25 Go away! (4,2)
26 Pay out (5)

DOWN

1 For nothing (6)
2 Ages (4)
3 Asian national (6)
4 Sketched (4)
5 Rows (5)
6 Clays (anag.) (5)
7 Liver disease (9)
8 Wed again (9)
11 Cheap wine (slang) (5)
12 Lo SOS! (anag.) (5)
16 Riot (6)
17 Type of shell (5)
18 Enlarge, widen (6)
19 Ascend (5)
22 Be off! (4)
23 SOS! (4)

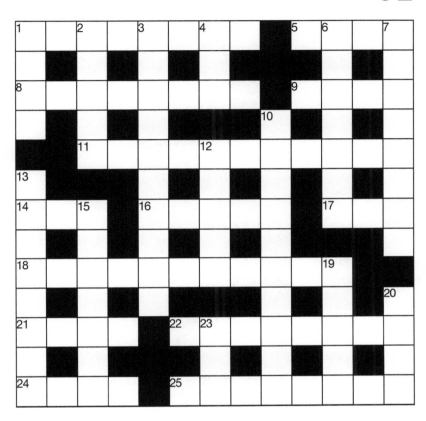

ACROSS

1 Diminish (8)
5 Zest (4)
8 Decrease (4,4)
9 Hades (4)
11 Considered (11)
14 Witch (3)
16 Wave (5)
17 Fitting (3)
18 Bitter (11)
21 Old (4)
22 Female pilot (8)
24 Farewell (2-2)
25 Liable to error (8)

DOWN

1 Filth (4)
2 Damon (anag.) (5)
3 Interfering (10)
4 Saying; cut wood (3)
6 Passiveness (7)
7 Iciness (8)
10 Brawl (4-3-3)
12 Nobleman (5)
13 Ant heaps (anag.) (8)
15 Vestment (7)
19 Cleanse (5)
20 Spindle (4)
23 Roman road (3)

32

ACROSS

1 Financial dealer (6)
4 Whip (5)
8 Oscillate (5)
9 Raise (7)
10 Left out (7)
11 Occident (4)
12 Hostelry (3)
14 Lake (4)
15 Always (4)
18 Forty winks (3)
21 Sole (4)
23 Visualise (7)
25 Tightly-knit (7)
26 Perfect (5)
27 Proportion (5)
28 Grab (6)

DOWN

1 Church dignitary (6)
2 Opening (7)
3 The genie (anag.) (8)
4 Retain (4)
5 Egg-shaped (5)
6 Score (6)
7 Composer of *La Traviata* (5)
13 Denial (8)
16 Distinguished (7)
17 Agree (6)
19 Ski-slope (5)
20 Well-being (6)
22 Boundary (5)
24 Aureole (4)

ACROSS

1 Longest UK river (6)
4 Grab (5)
8 Afro-Cuban dance (5)
9 Delighted (7)
10 Artist (7)
11 The Venerable —— (4)
12 Greek island (3)
14 A long time (4)
15 Blow (4)
18 Dump (3)
21 Pier (anag.) (4)
23 & 28 Pretentious manner (4,3,6)
25 Solicit votes (7)
26 Bingo (5)
27 Lowers head (5)
28 See 23

DOWN

1 Fragments (6)
2 Seducing and exploiting (colloq.) (7)
3 Start ode (anag.) (4-4)
4 Staunch (4)
5 Put into circulation (5)
6 Whirlpools (6)
7 Flash (5)
13 Firework (8)
16 Frenzied (7)
17 Detected (6)
19 Bedding plant (5)
20 Obnoxious (6)
22 Contagious fear (5)
24 Go by (4)

34

ACROSS

1 Dove's shelter (4)
4 Aircraft sheds (7)
8 Staunch (8)
9 Mate (3)
11 Vinegary (6)
13 Downright (6)
14 Luxurious (5)
15 Boot (4)
17 Torn (4)
18 Paris Underground (5)
20 Talisman (6)
21 Inuit (6)
24 Encountered (3)
25 A reading (anag.) (8)
26 Children's room (7)
27 Hard of hearing (4)

DOWN

2 Fantastic (5)
3 Cream pastry (6)
4 Practical joke (4)
5 Legal clerk (6)
6 Conciliate (7)
7 Greeting (10)
10 Board game (10)
12 Catlike mammal (5)
13 Sky-blue (5)
16 Oppose (7)
18 Paltry (6)
19 Belgian port (6)
22 Balearic island (5)
23 Conflict; wear at edges (4)

ACROSS

1 Three-piece —— (5)
4 Reveries (6)
9 Inquisitive (7)
10 Sir —— Ustinov (5)
11 Sees (anag.) (4)
12 Feeling (7)
13 Dog (3)
14 Nil (4)
16 eg Conger (4)
18 Rotten, evil (3)
20 Lying in court (7)
21 Maltese island (4)
24 A daughter of *Lear* (5)
25 Firedog (7)
26 Holy —— (6)
27 Upper air (5)

DOWN

1 Football (6)
2 Legendary Welsh giant (5)
3 Public school (4)
5 Rebuked (8)
6 All thin (anag.) (3-4)
7 Malay skirt (6)
8 Michaelmas daisy (5)
13 Pillar-shaped (8)
15 Infuriated (7)
17 Portuguese city (6)
18 Local authority regulation (5)
19 Angle; nook (6)
22 —— Winfrey (TV) (5)
23 Rim; advantage (4)

36

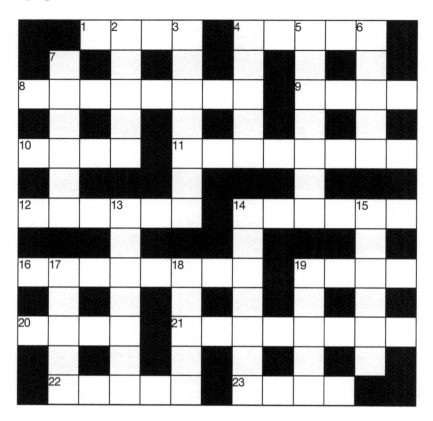

ACROSS

1 Recognise (4)
4 —— Mountains, in the south-east of America (5)
8 In pairs (3,2,3)
9 Sacred bird (4)
10 Whirlpool (4)
11 Acts (8)
12 Untouched (6)
14 *Old Testament* mount (6)
16 eg Rudolph (8)
19 Flag (4)
20 Insect (4)
21 Scoot, run! (anag.) (8)
22 Aromatic plant (5)
23 Otherwise (4)

DOWN

2 Worthily (5)
3 Lacking (7)
4 Bracing air (5)
5 —— *and the Forty Thieves* (3,4)
6 Blade (5)
7 European country (6)
13 Yearly plants (7)
14 Put in order (7)
15 Beehive (6)
17 From the books of (abbrev.) (2,3)
18 Surpass (5)
19 Solid (anag.) (5)

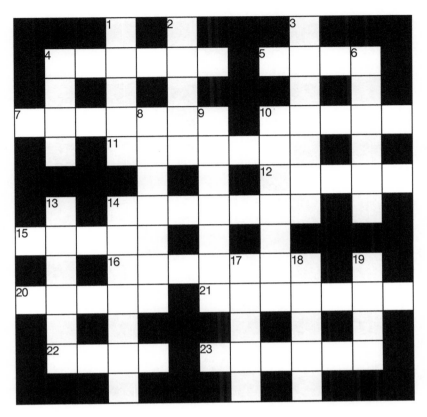

ACROSS

4 Japan (6)
5 Friar of Sherwood (4)
7 Wavy (7)
10 Middle part (5)
11 Yellow-flowered plant popularly known as Aaron's rod (7)
12 Twist (5)
14 Ordinary soldier (7)
15 Musical drama (5)
16 Oppressive (7)
20 A soft white rock (5)
21 Christmas fuel (4-3)
22 Chinese guild (4)
23 Expire (6)

DOWN

1 Drug (5)
2 Magnate (5)
3 River in southern France (7)
4 Ingenuous (4)
6 Destiny (6)
8 Excel (7)
9 Drudgery (7)
10 Pensive (7)
13 Result (6)
14 Draw out (7)
17 Route (anag.) (5)
18 Cuttlefish ink (5)
19 The two (4)

38

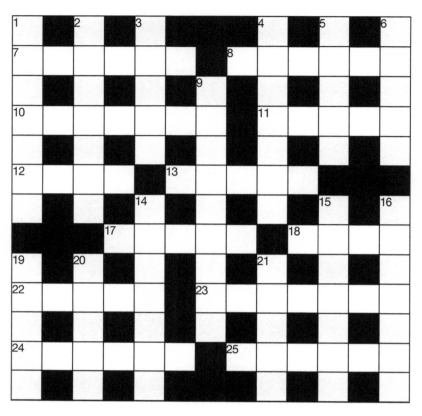

ACROSS

7 Confederacy (6)
8 Supporters (6)
10 Assemble (7)
11 Astonish (5)
12 Notion (4)
13 Donated (5)
17 Humped animal (5)
18 Masculine (4)
22 Airy; luminescence (5)
23 Abbreviate (7)
24 Secret vote (6)
25 Keep (6)

DOWN

1 Flabby (7)
2 Artist (7)
3 Silent (5)
4 Begged (7)
5 Opponent (5)
6 Deathly pale (5)
9 Dire scene (anag.) (9)
14 Heading (7)
15 Home on wheels (7)
16 Refuse (7)
19 Orb (5)
20 Spry (5)
21 Fibre (anag.) (5)

ACROSS

1 Comfort (6)
7 Sluggers (7)
8 Moan (8)
9 Speak (5)
10 Approaches (5)
11 Otherwise (4)
12 Borders (5)
15 Large ship (5)
16 Setting (5)
19 The Orient (4)
20 Woodwind instruments (5)
21 Interval (5)
22 An unspecified object (8)
23 Shedding skin (7)
24 Branches (6)

DOWN

1 Infirmity (8)
2 Berate severely (8)
3 Summons (5)
4 Wrongdoing (3)
5 Declared (6)
6 Light wind (6)
7 Sleeping in winter (11)
9 Exploiter (4)
13 Salutation (8)
14 eg Hot-dogs (8)
15 Let in water (4)
17 Part of eye (6)
18 Tidily (6)
20 Quotient (5)
22 Insect (3)

40

ACROSS

1 Convenient (5)
4 Surpassed (6)
9 *Hamlet*'s country (7)
10 Intends; wealth (5)
11 Get up (4)
12 Ancestry (7)
13 Boring tool (3)
14 Healthy (4)
16 Slaughtered (4)
18 First note of scale (3)
20 Setback (7)
21 Type of music (4)
24 London concerts (5)
25 Raiment (7)
26 Posted (anag.) (6)
27 Pacific island group (5)

DOWN

1 Ivy (6)
2 Roman date (5)
3 Twelvemonth (4)
5 Reprove (8)
6 Appease (7)
7 Walt —— , animator (6)
8 Cranium (5)
13 In the open (8)
15 Oi, Venus (anag.) (7)
17 Moaned constantly (6)
18 French impressionist (5)
19 Ericaceous plant (6)
22 Moses' brother (5)
23 Petty quarrel (4)

ACROSS

1 Michael —— (TV) (5)
4 Bury (5)
10 Reposing (7)
11 Nick (5)
12 Confess (5)
13 Untried (anag.) (7)
15 St Columba's island (4)
17 Make contact with (5)
19 Elector (5)
22 Thing (4)
25 Caller (7)
27 Insinuate (5)
29 Elephant tusks (5)
30 A hydrocarbon gas (7)
31 Apart (5)
32 Employing (5)

DOWN

2 Indian tea area (5)
3 Daft (7)
5 Tenon (anag.) (5)
6 Force out (7)
7 Dairy product (5)
8 Once more (5)
9 Tribal head (5)
14 Part of church (4)
16 American state (4)
18 Bony (7)
20 Inauspicious (7)
21 Miss (5)
23 Excursions (5)
24 Funeral fires (5)
26 Played (5)
28 Unadorned (5)

42

ACROSS

1 Santa —— , capital of 25 (4)
4 Corn lot (anag.) (7)
8 Giving out (8)
9 Sink (3)
11 Musical note (6)
13 Out-of-date (3,3)
14 Swill (5)
15 To eat away (4)
17 Electronic junk-mail (4)
18 VII (5)
20 More clownish (6)
21 Bunny (6)
24 Jeer (3)
25 A Canary Island (8)
26 Spanish inquisitor (7)
27 Pay (4)

DOWN

2 South American dance (5)
3 Stringed instrument (6)
4 Inch (anag.) (4)
5 Minor criticism (6)
6 Wayside fruit (7)
7 Lawful (10)
10 Concertina (7-3)
12 Waterway (5)
13 Rosie (anag.) (5)
16 Comply (7)
18 Church official (6)
19 Thin (6)
22 Obscure (5)
23 Burden (4)

ACROSS

1 Tiny songbird (4)
5 Christmas (4)
7 Impressive (7)
8 Polaris (4,4)
10 Pier (anag.) (4)
12 Gentle (4)
14 Checked out (8)
16 Calamity (8)
17 Profit (4)
18 Cosy (4)
19 Wound wrappings (8)
22 Victory (7)
23 Crowd; service (4)
24 Always (4)

DOWN

1 Stinging insect (4)
2 Title (4)
3 Aware (8)
4 Male pig (4)
5 Longing (8)
6 Border; advantage (4)
9 Point of view (7)
11 Recipes (anag.) (7)
13 Board-game (8)
15 Rural economy (8)
18 Slender (4)
19 French cheese (4)
20 Dull pain (4)
21 Prison; agitation (4)

44

ACROSS

1 French capital (5)
4 Peaks (7)
8 Extinct bird (3)
9 Score at cricket (3)
10 Wild dog (5)
11 Minor actor (5)
12 Knotted; growled (7)
15 Spouse (4)
17 Emphasise (6)
19 eg Razorback (6)
22 Osculate (4)
24 Sorrow (7)
26 Leaves (5)
28 Command (5)
30 Employ (3)
31 Hatchet (3)
32 Mexican cloaks (7)
33 Austere (5)

DOWN

1 Cossets (7)
2 Respond (5)
3 Yells (7)
4 Truthful (6)
5 Asian country (5)
6 Female bird (3)
7 Tolerated (5)
13 Curtains (4)
14 Allow (3)
16 Requests (4)
18 Colour (3)
20 Unserviceable (7)
21 Oriental (7)
23 Comes forth (6)
24 Crouch (5)
25 Solid ground (5)
27 Effigy (5)
29 Cacophony (3)

ACROSS

1 Building block (5)
4 Astound (4)
7 Overtake (4)
8 eg Handel's *Messiah* (8)
9 People collectively (9)
10 *Oedipus* ——— , opera by Stravinsky (3)
12 Rank (6)
14 Ridicule (6)
16 Status ——— , heavy metal group (3)
18 Victorian Prime Minister (9)
21 Unwanted post (4,4)
22 Ill-mannered (4)
23 Like a buffoon (4)
24 Procession (5)

DOWN

1 Virtuoso (7)
2 Example (8)
3 Thumping in engine; rap (5)
4 Owls (anag.) (4)
5 Join (5)
6 Put on the alert; cautioned (6)
11 Benchmarks (8)
13 Monetary unit of the United States of America (6)
15 City in New Zealand (7)
17 Fleshy piece in throat (5)
19 Earthenware (5)
20 All right (4)

ACROSS

1 Suffer (5)
4 Destroyed (7)
8 Hone (7)
9 Sudden fright (5)
10 Troublemaking (5)
11 Word for word (7)
13 Begin (4)
15 Symbolise (6)
17 Hearth-guard (6)
20 Rummage (4)
22 Cross-country runner (7)
24 Elite (5)
26 Pried (5)
27 Obvious (7)
28 Largish bag (7)
29 Ravine (5)

DOWN

1 Moment (7)
2 Ringing sound (5)
3 Censure (7)
4 Edible shellfish (6)
5 Englishman abroad (5)
6 Relatives (7)
7 Relating to a duke (5)
12 Data (abbrev.) (4)
14 Funeral fire (4)
16 Sunshade (7)
18 Engraved design (7)
19 Return fixture (7)
21 Severe trial (6)
22 Intuitive feeling (5)
23 Subcontinent (5)
25 Surrey town (5)

ACROSS

1 —— *et la Bête* (Cocteau film) (2,5)
5 eg Edna Everage (4)
7 Ballads (5)
8 Liverpool's river (6)
10 Cairo's river (4)
11 Converted into unit trusts (8)
13 Make certain (6)
14 Alabama port (6)
17 Dispossession (8)
19 Versifier (4)
21 14-line verse (6)
22 John —— (19) (5)
23 Dick Van —— (films) (4)
24 Meissen (anag.) (7)

DOWN

1 LA, California (3,7)
2 Baubles, —— , and beads (7)
3 Deadly sin (4)
4 Stoat's fur (6)
5 Length of time (8)
6 Encounters (5)
9 Plugs (colloq.) (10)
12 Make-believe (8)
15 Air boss (anag.) (7)
16 Massachussetts' capital (6)
18 Dentine (5)
20 Read superficially (4)

48

ACROSS

1 British author (7)
5 Irish female singer (4)
7 Nap (5)
8 Ecclesiastical building (6)
10 Heath (4)
11 Indian prince (8)
13 Musical composition (6)
14 Aided (6)
17 Oval (8)
19 Eyelid sore (4)
21 Human soul (6)
22 Rhubarb genus (5)
23 Zing (4)
24 Rumbles (anag.) (7)

DOWN

1 Supervisor (10)
2 Rest in a horizontal position (3,4)
3 Zulu regiment (4)
4 Recant (anag.) (6)
5 Rivalled (8)
6 Cassava (5)
9 Wishful thinker (10)
12 Uncharacteristic (8)
15 Vegetable for flavouring (3-4)
16 Arm muscle (6)
18 Cotton thread (5)
20 German lady (4)

ACROSS

1 Seductress (5)
4 Sibling (6)
9 Parvenu (7)
10 Guide (5)
11 Spanish artist (4)
12 Trusting (7)
13 Lad (3)
14 Behindhand (4)
16 Require (4)
18 Appropriate (3)
20 Studying (7)
21 Eye infection (4)
24 Cereal (5)
25 Fast, flash (7)
26 Whole (6)
27 Give in (5)

DOWN

1 Smear (6)
2 Dangerous (5)
3 Ordered; without water (4)
5 Cheeky (8)
6 Adolescent (7)
7 Uncommon item (6)
8 Narrative (5)
13 Novice (8)
15 Obdurate (7)
17 Stout shoe (6)
18 Once more (5)
19 Impassioned (6)
22 Cater (anag.) (5)
23 Perceive (4)

50

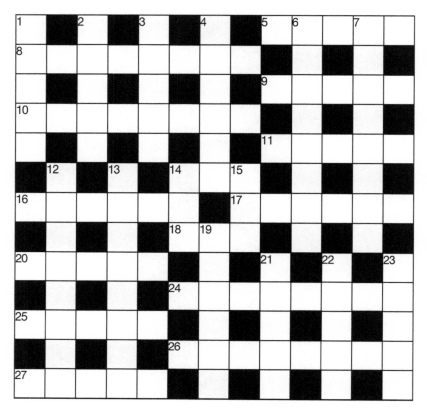

ACROSS

5 Drops (5)
8 Ten creep (anag.) (8)
9 Frighten (5)
10 Young hares (8)
11 Cutlery item (5)
14 Before (literary) (3)
16 Gasoline (6)
17 Guides (6)
18 Kind (3)
20 Chicken's noise (5)
24 Assassin (8)
25 *Fiddler on the Roof* star (5)
26 Head of the board (8)
27 Stow (5)

DOWN

1 Fruit (5)
2 Wait (5)
3 Fatigued (5)
4 Sea duck (6)
6 Taken (8)
7 Port (nautical) (8)
12 Betrays (5,3)
13 Affable (8)
14 *Old Testament* high priest (3)
15 River in the Borders (3)
19 Shows amusement (6)
21 Bill —— : birdwatcher (5)
22 Bread particle (5)
23 Bird; mechanical lift (5)

ACROSS

1 American acting awards (6)
7 Buddies (7)
8 Divine food (8)
9 Cant (5)
10 Question (5)
11 *Educating* —— , film (4)
12 Sanctions (5)
15 Fable writer (5)
16 Selenic (5)
19 Tale-teller (4)
20 Rum (5)
21 Staff of life (5)
22 Apron (8)
23 Huge gambling prize (7)
24 Somnolent (6)

DOWN

1 Peaceful (8)
2 Aristocrat (8)
3 Dark hardwood (5)
4 Age (3)
5 Waterproof jacket (6)
6 Serious crime (6)
7 eg Lime (6,5)
9 At the summit (4)
13 Lean poet (anag.) (8)
14 Hardly (8)
15 Parched (4)
17 Loud commotion (6)
18 Largest American state (6)
20 Game bird; flinch (5)
22 Ceramic vessel (3)

ACROSS

1 For what reason? (3)
3 Female deer (3)
5 William —— , Quaker (4)
7 Urge on (5)
8 Trinidad & —— (6)
10 Demure (4)
11 I stir cat (anag.) (8)
13 Strictness (6)
14 America's 50th state (6)
17 Designate (8)
19 Breathe hard (4)
21 —— Gardens, Copenhagen (6)
22 Civic leader (5)
23 Bench (4)
24 Dine (3)
25 Nineteenth letter (3)

DOWN

1 Speaking softly (10)
2 Barking (7)
3 Unemployment benefit (slang) (4)
4 To gain money by force (6)
5 Bar licensee (8)
6 Hours of darkness (5)
9 Sacred writings (10)
12 Was consumed by fire (5,3)
15 Any seal (anag.) (7)
16 Take a long step (6)
18 Corn (5)
20 Give off (4)

ACROSS

1 Sweat-gland opening (4)
4 Home (5)
8 Bird-watcher (8)
9 Observed (4)
10 Counter-tenor (4)
11 Terminate; deduce (8)
12 Of the skin (6)
14 Botch (6)
16 Latin and Greek (8)
19 Taunt (4)
20 Peruvian capital (4)
21 Hostile (8)
22 Laden (anag.) (5)
23 Chasm (4)

DOWN

2 Cap (5)
3 Moral (7)
4 eg Egret (5)
5 Greek "u" (7)
6 Correct text (5)
7 Dozen (6)
13 Eye make-up (7)
14 Sunbathing (7)
15 North African (6)
17 French river (5)
18 Greek epic (5)
19 Interrogate (5)

54

ACROSS

1 Understands (5)
5 Plunges (5)
8 Marine mammal (5)
9 Timely excuse (5)
10 Soliloquy (9)
11 Sarah (dim.) (3)
12 Just as far apart (11)
15 Impulse to steal (11)
19 Dance to pop music (3)
20 Recorder (9)
22 Academy Award (5)
23 Goodbye (5)
24 Full breakfast perhaps (3-2)
25 Agave fibre (5)

DOWN

1 Hiker's bag (8)
2 Yellow songbird (6)
3 Bathing-costume (8)
4 Tinned (6)
5 Wooded hollow (4)
6 Impotence drug (6)
7 Ides (anag.) (4)
13 Resonant (8)
14 Secular (8)
16 LXXX (6)
17 Swallow (6)
18 Old calculator (6)
20 Type of knot (4)
21 Detergent (4)

ACROSS

1 Rock-strewn (5)
4 Extravagantly ornate (7)
8 Business; worry (7)
9 Tyrone county town (5)
10 Edit (5)
11 Adjudicator (7)
13 Sicilian volcano (4)
15 Mock (6)
17 Root vegetable (6)
20 Mimicked (4)
22 Lament (7)
24 Expeditiousness (5)
26 Cited (anag.) (5)
27 Straits (7)
28 Substitute (5-2)
29 Fiend (5)

DOWN

1 Make good (7)
2 Snow-leopard (5)
3 Gave way (7)
4 Author of *Pilgrim's Progress* (6)
5 Diamond shape (5)
6 Fourth; mercy (7)
7 Clear upper air (5)
12 Competition (4)
14 Rip (4)
16 Duplicate (7)
18 Redhead (anag.) (7)
19 Crime against state (7)
21 Long narrow flag (6)
22 Actions (5)
23 Chose (5)
25 Tempest (5)

56

ACROSS

1 Pursue (6)
4 Brags (6)
7 Music tapes (9)
9 Humour (4)
10 Cicatrix (4)
11 Rips (5)
13 Metric volumes (6)
14 Wisest (6)
15 Warnings (6)
17 Allow (6)
19 Fills to satisfaction (5)
20 Snubs (4)
22 Recognised (4)
23 Hypothesising (9)
24 Thin paper (6)
25 Required (6)

DOWN

1 Conventional (6)
2 Burden (4)
3 Desires (6)
4 Electors (6)
5 Employs (4)
6 Hidden (6)
7 Shows differences (9)
8 Yelling (9)
11 Conditions (5)
12 Rescues (5)
15 eg Acute (6)
16 Specimen (6)
17 Individual (6)
18 In the direction of (6)
21 Takes to court (4)
22 Joint (4)

ACROSS

1 Boxing Day saint (7)
8 Purchasers (6)
9 Impedimenta (7)
11 Elitist universities (8)
12 Vendettas (5)
14 —— Fitzgerald, jazz (4)
15 Wasted (8)
17 Parvenus (8)
18 Sicilian volcano (4)
20 Blackboard-frame (5)
21 Useless material (8)
23 Non-aligned (7)
24 Chorister; multiply by three (6)
25 Hors d'oeuvre (7)

DOWN

2 Elates (anag.) (6)
3 Eastern temple (6)
4 *Cogito,* —— *sum* (4)
5 Water-plant (7)
6 Down-and-outs (9)
7 Indispensable (9)
10 Atonement (9)
12 Fruitfulness (9)
13 Cumbrian lake (9)
16 Cross roads carelessly (7)
18 Church festival (6)
19 Invalidate (6)
22 Nimble (4)

ACROSS

1 Small mammal (4)
4 Dried grape (6)
7 Scots "no" (3)
9 & 29 So to speak (2,2,4)
10 Flat voice (8)
11 French king (3)
12 eg Man, Wight (4)
13 —— acid (8)
16 Eminent (13)
19 Sailors (8)
23 Breezy (4)
24 Become unwell (3)
25 Worldly, secular (8)
26 Vole (anag.) (4)
27 Past, gone (3)
28 Stared fiercely (6)
29 See 9

DOWN

2 Murdered (12)
3 Beg (7)
4 Timer (anag.) (5)
5 Interior (5)
6 Within (prefix) (5)
8 Railway worker (6,6)
14 Fury (5)
15 —— chi: Chinese exercise system (3)
17 Hostelry (3)
18 Fork-tailed bird (7)
20 Urge forward (5)
21 Mistake (5)
22 Raw vegetable dish (5)

ACROSS

1 Pink-footed seabird (5)
4 Open by force (5)
10 Coaches, trains (7)
11 Slow learner (5)
12 Planet (5)
13 Antennae (7)
15 Jane Austen novel (4)
17 *The Mark of* —— (film) (5)
19 Stylish (slang) (5)
22 Somerset spa (4)
25 Sam, movie mogul (7)
27 Forefinger (5)
29 Possessed (5)
30 Answers (7)
31 Forge (anag.) (5)
32 Shattered (5)

DOWN

2 Different (5)
3 Sibling (7)
5 Horseman (5)
6 Sabbaths (7)
7 Court official (5)
8 Muslim religion (5)
9 Tantalise (5)
14 Compass point (4)
16 —— *Dick* by Herman Melville (4)
18 Florida resort (7)
20 Rumour (7)
21 Incite (3,2)
23 Inflamed (5)
24 Live (5)
26 Golf club (5)
28 Swallow (5)

60

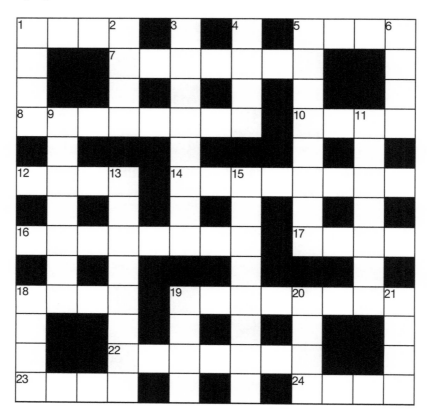

ACROSS

1 Keep sounding (4)
5 Deep ringing sound (4)
7 Happily (7)
8 Heated in an enclosed chamber (8)
10 Short stocking (4)
12 Scrutinise (4)
14 Wickedness (8)
16 Waterproof footwear (8)
17 Disconcert (4)
18 Muse of history (4)
19 Interpreter (8)
22 Facial feature (7)
23 Partly open (4)
24 People in general (4)

DOWN

1 Boiled pudding (4)
2 FBI agent (1-3)
3 Salty (8)
4 Breeze (4)
5 Substance used in staining (8)
6 Sticky material (4)
9 Rude (7)
11 Inhabitant (7)
13 Thinner (8)
15 Unskilled (8)
18 Unconscious state (4)
19 Pitcher (4)
20 Town (anag.) (4)
21 Wee (4)

ACROSS

1 Supplied with goods (7)
8 In pain (6)
9 All together (2,5)
11 Outside (8)
12 Fable writer (5)
14 Grain husks (4)
15 Appropriate (8)
17 Perfectionist (8)
18 Smudge (4)
20 Diving bird (5)
21 Unsuccessful (8)
23 Aroused (7)
24 Simply (6)
25 Vast (7)

DOWN

2 Sore (6)
3 Colouring pencil (6)
4 Gaelic (4)
5 Level of command (7)
6 Able to be separated (9)
7 Total (9)
10 Dear (9)
12 Renounced the throne (9)
13 Place of refuge (4,5)
16 Altogether (3,4)
18 Rubies (anag.) (6)
19 Preoccupy (6)
22 Test (4)

ACROSS

1 Apportion (5)
4 Middle Easterner (5)
10 Gaunt (7)
11 Din (5)
12 Cherubs (art) (5)
13 A Dumas musketeer (7)
15 Swear-word (4)
17 Force of blow (5)
19 Habituate (5)
22 Instrument (4)
25 Lithe (7)
27 Blame (anag.) (5)
29 Entitled (5)
30 Pick again (2-5)
31 Worship (5)
32 Apart (5)

DOWN

2 Illumination (5)
3 Speech (7)
5 Junior (5)
6 The rein (anag.) (7)
7 Hacks (5)
8 Skilful (5)
9 Untidy (5)
14 American state (4)
16 Small particle (4)
18 Took up again (7)
20 Makes less 9 (7)
21 Unseeing (5)
23 Fruit (5)
24 Dentition (5)
26 Command (5)
28 Food; money (5)

ACROSS

1 Football score (4)
4 Sumptuous (2,4)
7 Blade (rowing) (3)
9 Printing term (4)
10 Edible snail (8)
11 Light meal (3)
12 Look with desire (4)
13 Resting (8)
16 Reference book (13)
19 Pacts (8)
23 Make beer (4)
24 Lubricant (3)
25 Disadvantage (8)
26 Ingests (4)
27 Breed of dog (dim.) (3)
28 Rugged (6)
29 Brood (4)

DOWN

2 Person over 80 years of age (12)
3 Prize draw (7)
4 Gloomy and uninteresting (5)
5 Of the area (5)
6 Copy machine (5)
8 Simultaneous (12)
14 Wear away (5)
15 —— Khan; Turkish leader (3)
17 Crib (3)
18 Symbols (7)
20 Check accounts (5)
21 To bring upon oneself (5)
22 Over sentimental (5)

64

ACROSS

1 Spinal (anag.) (6)
4 Ceramicist (6)
7 Vanish (9)
9 Regrets (4)
10 Penetrating; ardent (4)
11 Fastener (5)
13 Delegate (6)
14 More trim (6)
15 Bee colony (6)
17 Tommy ——— , private (6)
19 Prematurely (5)
20 Watch (4)
22 Rebuff (4)
23 Plain-spoken (9)
24 Was inclined (6)
25 Tormentor (6)

DOWN

1 Rotten (6)
2 ——— Murdoch, novelist (4)
3 Not plentiful (6)
4 Marionette (6)
5 Hardwood (4)
6 Sprinter (6)
7 Lost hope (9)
8 Receiver (9)
11 Look hard (5)
12 Humorous (5)
15 Arrival (6)
16 Gaped (6)
17 Confederates (6)
18 Yield (6)
21 Timber (4)
22 Cast off (4)

ACROSS

1 Fail to hit (4)
5 French for "she" (4)
7 Wicked (7)
8 Bully (8)
10 Past (4)
12 Catch sight of (4)
14 Valuable hoard (8)
16 Aide-mémoire (8)
17 Certain (4)
18 Quiet call for attention (4)
19 Smoked, highly-seasoned cut of beef (8)
22 Musical piece (7)
23 Shop (anag.) (4)
24 Actual (4)

DOWN

1 Biblical kingdom (4)
2 Demonstrate (4)
3 Guided, superintended (8)
4 Almost all (4)
5 Marries, embraces (8)
6 At all times (4)
9 Put or keep down (7)
11 Rude ram (anag.) (7)
13 Three-part painting (8)
15 Pre-Roman Italian (8)
18 Support (4)
19 Small horse (4)
20 Bring up (4)
21 *Pop ——* (television) (4)

66

ACROSS

1 He, —— or it (3)
3 Belonging to him (3)
5 eg Ilkley, Othello (4)
7 Plump (5)
8 Stoned (6)
10 Rather ——
(preference) (4)
11 Blamed (8)
13 Spanner (6)
14 Handgun (6)
17 Mended (8)
19 Feline musical (4)
21 Lowly, modest (6)
22 Farewell (5)
23 Rim (4)
24 Drunkard (3)
25 Empty talk (colloq.) (3)

DOWN

1 Begins task (4,2,4)
2 Hug (7)
3 Welsh fervour (4)
4 Seven-piece band (6)
5 Bond between friends
in Australia (8)
6 Heavy blow or a big lie
(3-2)
9 Harem women (10)
12 Scrawl (8)
15 Tantalising (7)
16 Cuts (6)
18 Beat (5)
20 Handle (4)

ACROSS

1 Thorn (anag.) (5)
4 —— King, singer (6)
9 Ship (5)
10 English explorer (7)
11 Speech (7)
12 Surpass (5)
14 Cows chew it (3)
15 & 16 Orbiting space-station (3,3)
18 Knight's title (3)
21 Of sound (5)
22 One of three born together (7)
23 Drums (7)
25 Flexible (5)
26 Northern diocese (6)
27 Beg (5)

DOWN

1 Horatio ——, naval commander (6)
2 Pillaged (9)
3 Like a brave man (6)
5 Joined (6)
6 Broad Japanese sash (3)
7 Breathe out (6)
8 Old barrier between East & West Europe (4,7)
13 Fruit dish (9)
17 —— & raved (6)
18 Piece of music (6)
19 Stimulus (6)
20 Be there (6)
24 Spoil (3)

68

ACROSS

1 Strong emotion (7)
5 Wheat powder (5)
8 Sidestep (5)
9 Latin dance (7)
10 Homer —— (television cartoon) (7)
11 South American animal (5)
12 Jumbled mass (6)
14 Take on (6)
17 Schoolgirl's dress (5)
19 Uncommitted (7)
22 Stick out (7)
23 Bodily faculty (5)
24 Slide (anag.) (5)
25 Country properties (7)

DOWN

1 Mountain tops (5)
2 Icy figure (7)
3 Pakistani river (5)
4 Stockings (6)
5 Handles clumsily (7)
6 —— Beach (D-Day, World War Two) (5)
7 What CAMRA wants (4,3)
12 Walks unsteadily (7)
13 Talk (7)
15 Erect (7)
16 Addition to building (6)
18 Distinguished (5)
20 Overturn, spill (5)
21 Thin strips of wood (5)

ACROSS

1 Continue (5,2)
8 Tidier (6)
9 Conduit (7)
11 Amorous (8)
12 Slumber (5)
14 Look after (4)
15 Motorboats (8)
17 Fiscal (8)
18 Former (4)
20 Egged on (5)
21 Drapes (8)
23 Sorrow (7)
24 Motor (6)
25 Counts (on) (7)

DOWN

2 For a short time (6)
3 Hired (6)
4 Finished (4)
5 Stays behind (7)
6 Sewing (9)
7 Refined (of food) (9)
10 Sites (9)
12 Extended (9)
13 Spur on (9)
16 Drug, crack (7)
18 Citrus fruit (6)
19 Stopped (6)
22 Rescue (4)

ACROSS

1 Mohammed's birthplace (5)
4 Notches (5)
10 Front tooth (7)
11 Tag (5)
12 Musical work (5)
13 Violent attack (7)
15 Travelled by bike (4)
17 Dutch cheese (5)
19 Astound (5)
22 Yarn (4)
25 Elation (7)
27 Aspirated letter (5)
29 Schemes (5)
30 Renault (anag.) (7)
31 Racing venue (5)
32 Spartan slave (5)

DOWN

2 Compère (5)
3 Sweet sauce (7)
5 Lazes (5)
6 Israeli commune (7)
7 Intolerant person (5)
8 Terror (5)
9 Bombardment (5)
14 Aquatic mammal (4)
16 Swear-word (4)
18 French city (7)
20 Act; rule (7)
21 Expert (5)
23 Expiate (5)
24 Edible mollusc (5)
26 Zest (5)
28 Trunk (5)

ACROSS

1 More ill (6)
4 Swoon (5)
8 Crucifix (5)
9 eg Slates, thatch (7)
10 Boards ship (7)
11 Monster (4)
12 Pig (3)
14 Smile broadly (4)
15 Ready to eat (4)
18 Firearm (3)
21 Licentious party (4)
23 Collapse inwards (7)
25 Chilli sauce (7)
26 Holiday isle (5)
27 Beatle Starr (5)
28 Concurred (6)

DOWN

1 Football (6)
2 Hit; gear (slang) (7)
3 Making safe (8)
4 Amphibian (4)
5 Cake frosting (5)
6 Labelled (6)
7 Flashy, crude (5)
13 Grasping (8)
16 PR video (anag.) (7)
17 Luggage-carrier (6)
19 Ex-American president (5)
20 —— Ford, ex-American president (6)
22 African country (5)
24 Norwegian city (4)

ACROSS

1 Swiss villa (6)
7 Seasons (7)
8 Greek sea-god (8)
9 Film (America) (5)
10 Manuel de ——
(composer) (5)
11 Welsh emblem (4)
12 Revolt (5)
15 —— Lee (slang) (5)
16 Sports venue (5)
19 Always (4)
20 Voter (anag.) (5)
21 Move to music (5)
22 Hallucinatory drug (8)
23 Discusses (7)
24 Entreaty (6)

DOWN

1 Face pout (anag.) (3,2,3)
2 Unlimited (8)
3 Heather (5)
4 Spirit (3)
5 Blow (6)
6 Laud (6)
7 American baseball
matches (5,6)
9 Pool (4)
13 East Yorkshire minster
(8)
14 Hearer (8)
15 Talk wildly (4)
17 Lecturer (6)
18 Delicious drink (6)
20 Happen (5)
22 —— Gibson (actor) (3)

ACROSS

1 Elevated (4)
4 Line (5)
8 Liquefy (8)
9 Bog fuel (4)
10 Swelling disease (4)
11 Ship's officers' mess (8)
12 Clever (6)
14 Binary (anag.) (6)
16 Result of division sum (8)
19 Droop (4)
20 Siamese (4)
21 Medicinal plant (8)
22 Royal (5)
23 Sea-foam (4)

DOWN

2 Tines (anag.) (5)
3 Fool (7)
4 —— Street (5)
5 Trading centres (7)
6 Muse of lyric love poetry (5)
7 Strictness (6)
13 *Air on a* —— (1-6)
14 Soon (7)
15 Jocular word for head (6)
17 Doorkeeper (5)
18 Outshine (5)
19 Thighbone (5)

ACROSS

1 Dry (of wine) (3)
3 Cunning (3)
5 Rock grains (4)
7 Film cassette (5)
8 Taiwan capital (6)
10 Hindu god (4)
11 Interfering (8)
13 Solar system model (6)
14 Itinerant salesman (6)
17 Sideways (8)
19 Aeons (4)
21 Re bias (anag.) (6)
22 Italian isle (5)
23 Medal (slang) (4)
24 Dingy brown (3)
25 eg Carmelite (3)

DOWN

1 Economises (5,5)
2 Corpse (7)
3 Dot, stain (4)
4 Chatter incessantly (Scots) (6)
5 Defrauded (8)
6 Birthmarks (5)
9 Hostile action (10)
12 English poet (8)
15 Cricket ball (3-4)
16 Dances (anag.) (6)
18 Reclusive film star (5)
20 Scrutinise; glance over (4)

ACROSS

1 The length of (5)
4 Raise anchor (5)
10 Flexible (7)
11 Domesticates (5)
12 Lariat (5)
13 Knotted (7)
15 Want (4)
17 Light wood (5)
19 Bottomless pit (5)
22 Identical (4)
25 Get better (7)
27 Literary play (5)
29 Undercover agents (5)
30 Abdomen (7)
31 Join together (5)
32 Produce metal by heat (5)

DOWN

2 Inclines (5)
3 Ideas (7)
5 Consumed (5)
6 Bets (7)
7 Screams (5)
8 Extremely intense (5)
9 Whispered comment (5)
14 First man (4)
16 Relaxation (4)
18 Public sale by bid (7)
20 Dormitory (7)
21 Get hold of (5)
23 Get to one's feet (5)
24 Sailboat (5)
26 Call on (5)
28 Be of use (5)

ACROSS

1 Manipulates (7)
5 Played slowly (5)
8 Truck (5)
9 Snakelike (7)
10 Self-gratifying action (3-4)
11 Produce young (5)
12 Expensive (6)
14 Stern (6)
17 Citrus fruit (5)
19 Lewd (7)
22 Hermit (7)
23 Play (5)
24 Adjusted frequency (5)
25 Small axe (7)

DOWN

1 Split in two (5)
2 Apprehensive (7)
3 Early (anag.) (5)
4 Large prawns (6)
5 Easily read (7)
6 German river (5)
7 Late (7)
12 Guilty party (7)
13 Lethargic (7)
15 Nonsense (3-4)
16 Jacob's favourite (6)
18 Burgundian wine (5)
20 Former Egyptian president (5)
21 Precise (5)

ACROSS

1 June ——— , Hollywood musical star (7)
5 *A Fish Called* ——— : film (5)
8 African antelope (5)
9 Lewis ——— , author (7)
10 Expiation (9)
12 Clinging plant (3)
13 Meal (6)
14 Flogged (6)
17 Atmosphere (3)
18 Mail price (anag.) (9)
20 Dogged (7)
21 Corners (5)
23 Terror (5)
24 Poet (7)

DOWN

1 Stadium (5)
2 Meadow (3)
3 Sorrow (7)
4 An American coin (6)
5 Direst (5)
6 Stone Age (9)
7 Quelled (7)
11 Convenient (9)
13 Attained (7)
15 Rare nag (anag.) (7)
16 Card suit (6)
18 Finished (5)
19 Vigorous (5)
22 Fuel (3)

78

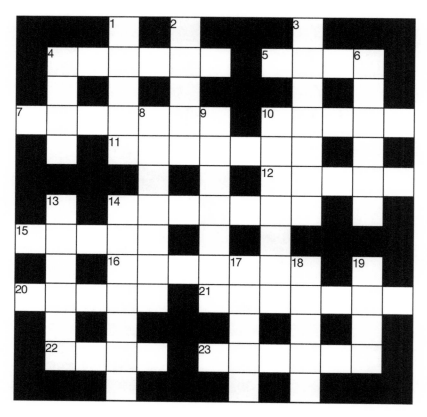

ACROSS

4 —— Piggott (jockey) (6)
5 Swiss psychiatrist (4)
7 Bonnie Prince —— (7)
10 Hooded coat (5)
11 Will Leo? (anag.) (3,4)
12 Wide-awake (5)
14 Illogical argument (7)
15 Treatment for addicts (abbrev.) (5)
16 White ant (7)
20 Wide (5)
21 Wave (7)
22 Eye greedily (4)
23 Fisherman (6)

DOWN

1 ——physics, study of interstellar matter (5)
2 Danger (5)
3 Via the ear (7)
4 Bert ——, Lion in *The Wizard of Oz* (4)
6 Low racing vehicle (2-4)
8 Late riser (3-4)
9 Web meal (anag.) (3-4)
10 Appease (7)
13 An eccentric (slang) (6)
14 Mortally (7)
17 Satire, sarcasm (5)
18 Noblemen (5)
19 Rip (4)

ACROSS

1 Short skirt (4)
4 Shoal (6)
7 Kernel (3)
9 Deer (4)
10 Unskilful; genuine (8)
11 Fabulous bird (3)
12 Killer-whale (4)
13 Chief element (8)
16 Miserly (5-8)
19 Forever (8)
23 Hood (4)
24 Choose (3)
25 Ill-balanced (8)
26 Tray (anag.) (4)
27 Listener (3)
28 Necessitate (6)
29 EU money (4)

DOWN

2 Motorway junction (12)
3 Impress deeply (7)
4 Unable to move (5)
5 Weighty (5)
6 Group of eight (5)
8 eg Flowing river (7,5)
14 Eject (5)
15 Bag (3)
17 Over there (3)
18 Metric area (7)
20 Having got up (5)
21 Subcontinent (5)
22 Sing partly falsetto (5)

80

ACROSS

1 Bring about (5)
4 Nettle (5)
10 Pacific islands (7)
11 More than enough (5)
12 Trap (5)
13 Secured (anag.) (7)
15 Vehicle on runners (4)
17 Pursue (5)
19 Heartbreak (5)
22 Duelling sword (4)
25 Call together (7)
27 Walk proudly (5)
29 Toss (5)
30 Faultfinding (7)
31 Chalcedony (5)
32 Gem (5)

DOWN

2 Scene of conflict (5)
3 Cloudy (7)
5 Rips (5)
6 Roman sea god (7)
7 Elk (5)
8 Mother-of-pearl (5)
9 Prepared (5)
14 Lip; advantage (4)
16 Welsh emblem (4)
18 Pendent (7)
20 Book; store (7)
21 Jeer (5)
23 Cheap (anag.) (5)
24 The boards (5)
26 Should (5)
28 Elevate (5)

ACROSS

1 Merry, festive (5)
4 Messing about on the water? (7)
8 If (7)
9 Musical drama (5)
10 Greek letter (5)
11 Alternatives (7)
13 Express choice (4)
15 Value highly (6)
17 Matched (6)
20 & 27 Public school (4,7)
22 Sea-god (7)
24 Public school; sport (5)
26 Assists (5)
27 See 20
28 Kitchen unit surface (7)
29 Extinct birds (5)

DOWN

1 A new job (anag.) (7)
2 Belgian city (5)
3 —— -ho (song) (2-5)
4 Brigitte —— , 1950s sex kitten (6)
5 Nearly (5)
6 Polar ship (7)
7 Clutches (5)
12 South American coin (4)
14 Portent (4)
16 Boozer (7)
18 Run duel (anag.) (7)
19 Aridity (7)
21 Storm in a —— (6)
22 Never (colloq.) (5)
23 Overturn (5)
25 Gluttony (5)

82

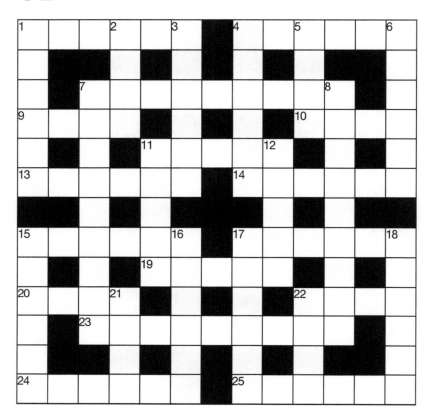

ACROSS

1 Supported (6)
4 Weirder (6)
7 Micro-organism (9)
9 Legal right (4)
10 Cultivate (4)
11 Perfume (5)
13 Stump (6)
14 Military show (6)
15 Fulmar (anag.) (6)
17 Smooth (6)
19 Film (5)
20 Micro-organism (4)
22 Castle (4)
23 Commotion (9)
24 Tic (6)
25 Roman military body (6)

DOWN

1 Wave (6)
2 Persian governor (4)
3 Discover (6)
4 Roving (6)
5 Crushing defeat (4)
6 Venetian bridge (6)
7 Reference point (9)
8 Parasitic plant (9)
11 Watery liquid (5)
12 Board (5)
15 Month (6)
16 Bath scrubber (6)
17 Spasmodic (6)
18 Italian painter (6)
21 Thaw (4)
22 Lash (4)

ACROSS

1 Pleasantly pungent (7)
5 Masticates (5)
8 Separately (5)
9 Summary; debilitated (3-4)
10 Total possessions (7)
11 Throw out (5)
12 Modernise (6)
14 Northern Ireland (6)
17 Serious (5)
19 Pragmatist (7)
22 Show (7)
23 Compare (5)
24 Discrimination (5)
25 Remains (7)

DOWN

1 Position (5)
2 Drank (7)
3 Room at the top (5)
4 Soundly defeat; party (6)
5 Hide (7)
6 Wear away (5)
7 Treason (anag.) (7)
12 Ointment (7)
13 Quiver (7)
15 Bamboozled (7)
16 Public speaker (6)
18 Greenfly (5)
20 Collection of maps (5)
21 Strained (5)

84

ACROSS

1 Moneybag (5)
4 Harsh (6)
9 Farm vehicle (7)
10 Colander (5)
11 Curse (4)
12 Intransigent (7)
13 Vague (3)
14 Renown (4)
16 Scintilla (4)
18 Part of circle (3)
20 Complicated (7)
21 Serene (4)
24 Kitchen garment (5)
25 Treat cruelly (7)
26 Dwell (6)
27 Rituals (5)

DOWN

1 Large snake (6)
2 Cook in oven (5)
3 Consumes (4)
5 Rapturous (8)
6 Graceful (7)
7 Chooses (6)
8 Aspiration (5)
13 Refused (8)
15 Looks up to (7)
17 Long, individual cake (6)
18 Maxim (5)
19 Entertains (6)
22 Warn (5)
23 Prod (4)

85

ACROSS

1 Exclamation of relief (4)
4 Kent resort (7)
8 Muddled (8)
9 Spurt (3)
11 Abusive remark (6)
13 Unsystematic (6)
14 —— Flynn, actor (5)
15 Row in theatre (4)
17 eg Big Ben (4)
18 Corn goddess (5)
20 Account (6)
21 Grading; sailor (6)
24 Rower (3)
25 Sufficient (8)
26 Edith —— , poet (7)
27 Entice (4)

DOWN

2 Rings to go through? (5)
3 Verbiage (6)
4 Disguise (4)
5 Sort of tyre (6)
6 Decide; award (7)
7 Study of insects (10)
10 Triumphant (10)
12 Sampled (5)
13 Dog's name (5)
16 Passage from book (7)
18 Make (6)
19 *Old Testament* prophet (6)
22 Bury (5)
23 Enthusiasm (4)

86

ACROSS

1 —— Nin, author (5)
4 Truman ——, writer (6)
9 Canadian province (7)
10 Gird one's —— (5)
11 Pleasant (4)
12 May diet (anag.) (7)
13 Donkey (3)
14 Drop (4)
16 Facial organ (4)
18 Horse (3)
20 —— Dietrich (7)
21 Festivity (4)
24 Line dance (5)
25 Not tested (7)
26 Israeli currency (6)
27 Bit (5)

DOWN

1 Sum (6)
2 Upper room (5)
3 Aching (4)
5 Quelling, calming (8)
6 So I grin (anag.) (7)
7 Follows (6)
8 —— and chattels (5)
13 Estrange (8)
15 Settle, work out (7)
17 Spanks (6)
18 Bond; linked group (5)
19 Canoe oar (6)
22 Get up (5)
23 Halt (4)

ACROSS

1 Sussex resort (4)
4 WW1 battle (6)
7 eg Corporal (1,1,1)
9 Performs (4)
10 Dominion, authority (8)
11 Employ (3)
12 Soviet Union (1,1,1,1)
13 Irritable (8)
16 Virtuous QEI (4,5,4)
19 Transfer (4,4)
23 Sea duck (4)
24 Operations room (3)
25 Channel isle (8)
26 York's river (4)
27 Murmur softly (3)
28 Stick (6)
29 Food (slang) (4)

DOWN

2 Now and then (12)
3 Made certain (7)
4 Rodents (5)
5 Less common (5)
6 Overturn (5)
8 Assist heroes (anag.) (12)
14 Cheshire rail junction (5)
15 Girl's name (3)
17 Status —— (3)
18 Wind instrument (7)
20 Awe (5)
21 Meeting place (5)
22 Rolls- —— (5)

88

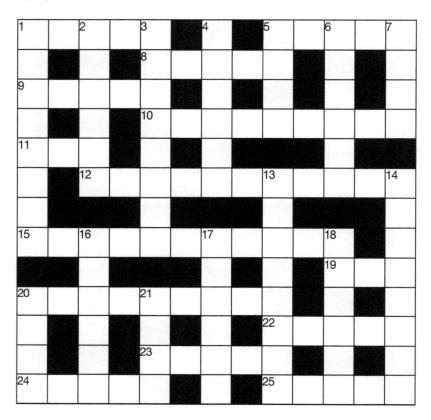

ACROSS

1 & 5 Resort in Monaco (5,5)
8 Measuring rod (5)
9 Farewell (5)
10 Possible (9)
11 Extra run in cricket (3)
12 Tidy curates (anag.) (5-6)
15 Disputably (11)
19 Umberto ——— , writer (3)
20 Sports vehicle (6,3)
22 Assault (5)
23 Stuffing (5)
24 Steed (5)
25 North African country (5)

DOWN

1 Rissole (8)
2 Spread by rumours (6)
3 Bursting out (8)
4 Showy (6)
5 Measure of herrings (4)
6 Oppose (6)
7 Elliptical (4)
13 Upward line in writing (8)
14 Electrical controller (8)
16 ——— -tape machine (6)
17 Hold; tenant (6)
18 Frothy (6)
20 *Old Testament* book (4)
21 Nuclear weapon (slang) (4)

ACROSS

1 Shorter (6)
4 Grab (5)
8 Gun; plunder (5)
9 Function (7)
10 Spoiling (7)
11 Lake (4)
12 Strike (3)
14 Network (4)
15 Counter-tenor (4)
18 Pull along (3)
21 Screen; skin (4)
23 Sealegs (anag.) (7)
25 Love-story (7)
26 Forbidden (5)
27 Uncaring gesture (5)
28 Stick (6)

DOWN

1 Metallic element (6)
2 Umpire (7)
3 Vision (8)
4 West (anag.) (4)
5 Stupid (5)
6 Soccer team (6)
7 Branch (5)
13 Possessing aptitude (8)
16 Quiver (7)
17 Maps; plans (6)
19 Vacillate (5)
20 On land (6)
22 Raise objection (5)
24 Difficulty (4)

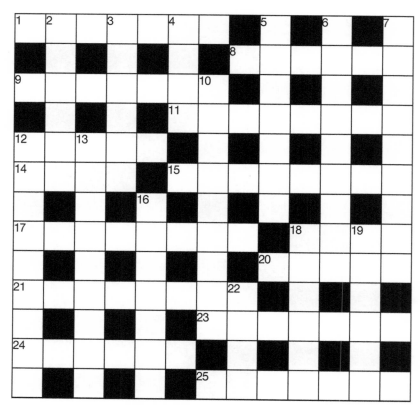

ACROSS

1 Oracle (7)
8 Touch lightly (6)
9 Transport contractor (7)
11 Banter (8)
12 Dying coal (5)
14 Ruse (anag.) (4)
15 Jointly (8)
17 Appalled (8)
18 Small biting fly (4)
20 Bird of prey (5)
21 Kept apart (8)
23 Main meals (7)
24 Improves (6)
25 Wood particles (7)

DOWN

2 Kingdoms (6)
3 Steal (6)
4 Pitcher (4)
5 Mosque tower (7)
6 Drawing roughly (9)
7 Rejoice (9)
10 Recuperated (9)
12 Extolled (9)
13 German composer (9)
16 Dangers (7)
18 Earned (6)
19 Warns (6)
22 Prima donna (4)

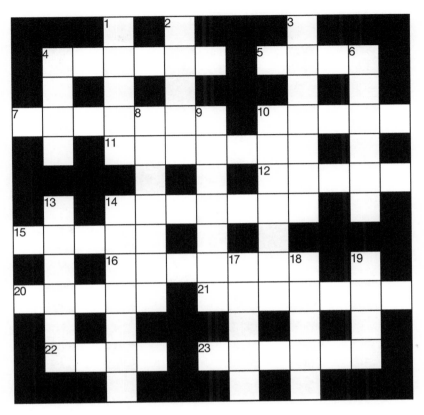

ACROSS

4 Frolic (6)
5 Goes astray (4)
7 Country-lover (7)
10 Pilfer (5)
11 Renegade (7)
12 Irritated (5)
14 Weird (7)
15 Ski-slope (5)
16 North-west African capital (7)
20 Cautious (5)
21 Pungent pepper (7)
22 Remove skin (4)
23 Soft felt hat (6)

DOWN

1 Bright; sting (5)
2 Beverage (5)
3 Grassy plain (7)
4 Tackle (4)
6 Fired (6)
8 Angrily (7)
9 Colossal (7)
10 Fraudulent copy (7)
13 Chess piece (6)
14 Jumped (7)
17 Agree (anag.) (5)
18 Spanish title (5)
19 Native Peruvian (4)

ACROSS

1 Sightless (5)
4 Dawdle (5)
10 Calls to appear (7)
11 *Lorna* —— : novel (5)
12 Additional (5)
13 Capture, trap (7)
15 Ripped (4)
17 Gluttony (5)
19 Dwelling (5)
22 Tropical fruit (4)
25 Wordy (7)
27 Undress (5)
29 Western show (5)
30 Dubious (2,5)
31 Employers (5)
32 Deathly pale (5)

DOWN

2 Sidney —— , films (5)
3 New baby (7)
5 South American range (5)
6 Spotted cat (7)
7 Willow (5)
8 Cinema attendant (5)
9 Verse (anag.) (5)
14 Tidy (4)
16 Chances (4)
18 Altar screen (7)
20 Moreover (7)
21 Evident (5)
23 Patronage (5)
24 Flood (5)
26 Smell (5)
28 Awaken (5)

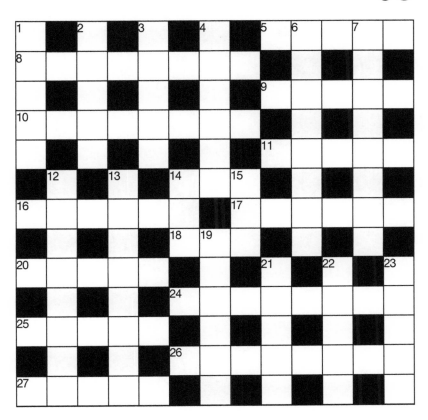

ACROSS

5 Artillery salute (5)
8 Of late (8)
9 Swoon (5)
10 Crucial (8)
11 Wild (5)
14 Divan (3)
16 Man's hat (6)
17 Concurs (6)
18 Sweet potato (3)
20 eg Maine (5)
24 Two-humped camel (8)
25 Writhe (5)
26 Chew the cud (8)
27 Side-road (5)

DOWN

1 Smart (5)
2 Loft (5)
3 Deserve (5)
4 Corruption (6)
6 Dilettantes (8)
7 Gave tins (anag.) (8)
12 eg Crusoe (8)
13 Disney film (8)
14 Botany or Biscay, for example (3)
15 eg Aswan (3)
19 Counting-frame (6)
21 Uncomplaining (5)
22 Northern Italian city (5)
23 Scornful expression (5)

94

ACROSS

1 —— of Athens (5)
4 Proposal (6)
9 Scrutinises (7)
10 Young eel (5)
11 Peeress (4)
12 Cold-blooded animal (7)
13 Peak; child's toy (3)
14 Extinct bird (4)
16 Dull pain (4)
18 Shed tears (3)
20 Prize draw (7)
21 Oast (anag.) (4)
24 Tenet (5)
25 Wool-fat (7)
26 Rover (6)
27 Yawned (5)

DOWN

1 Struggle (6)
2 Pile (5)
3 Tack (4)
5 Exaggerate (8)
6 Revile (7)
7 Gave strength (6)
8 Seize wrongfully (5)
13 Endure (8)
15 Eight-sided figure (7)
17 Motorless plane (6)
18 Go by bike (5)
19 Cautioned (6)
22 Flowering bulb (5)
23 Obstacle (4)

ACROSS

1 Col; impudence (4)
3 Casseroles (8)
9 Sculpt (5)
10 Withholding of information (5-2)
11 Uncooked (3)
13 Hopeless (9)
14 Hunnish conqueror (6)
16 Cowboy's rope (6)
18 Vapid (9)
20 Age (3)
22 Stretchy (7)
23 Depart (5)
25 Take avoiding action (8)
26 Talk (4)

DOWN

1 Pleasanter (5)
2 Private transport (3)
4 Cut out (6)
5 Mediterranean resort area (7)
6 Story (9)
7 Wise (7)
8 Require (4)
12 Resist (9)
14 Horns (7)
15 Ophelia's brother (7)
17 Secure (anag.) (6)
19 Vend (4)
21 Representative (5)
24 Tree; remains (3)

96

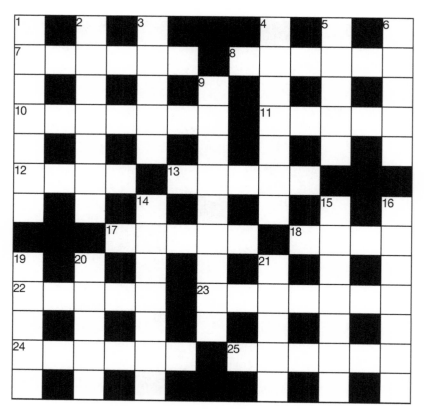

ACROSS

7 From side to side of (6)
8 Adheres (6)
10 Stately home (7)
11 Commerce (5)
12 Vend (4)
13 Notch; twenty (5)
17 Pry (5)
18 Lofty (4)
22 More up-to-date (5)
23 Beg (7)
24 Very little; time (6)
25 Awkward (6)

DOWN

1 Fortune-teller (7)
2 Tip; furrow (7)
3 Moving (5)
4 Height (7)
5 Throw away; fight (5)
6 Enquired (5)
9 Noted case (anag.) (9)
14 Fib (7)
15 Predicament (7)
16 Sleep (4-3)
19 Foe (5)
20 Show off (5)
21 Stem; follow (5)

ACROSS

1 Fresh (3)
3 Tier (3)
5 Oceans (4)
7 eg the Scillies (5)
8 Allowance (6)
10 Punch in boxing (4)
11 Interrogate (8)
13 American pacific state (6)
14 OK for eating (6)
17 eg Luther (8)
19 Seep (4)
21 Social calls (6)
22 Rotas (anag.) (5)
23 Ruffian (4)
24 Levy (3)
25 Termination (3)

DOWN

1 People next door (10)
2 Warm reception (7)
3 Chance (4)
4 Preliminary exercise (4-2)
5 Land taken out of production (3-5)
6 Garlic mayonnaise (5)
9 Attentive (10)
12 Board for advertisements (8)
15 Patterned fabric (7)
16 Fast-living group (3,3)
18 Trust (5)
20 Antelope (4)

98

ACROSS

1 The Ram (5)
4 Car for holiday trip (6)
9 Strong lever (7)
10 Meter (5)
11 Scottish island (4)
12 Charming (7)
13 Block of paper (3)
14 Wail (4)
16 Sliding frame (4)
18 Choose (3)
20 Huge (7)
21 Fall in small amounts (4)
24 Game with 40 cards (5)
25 Thing (7)
26 Spin round (6)
27 Senior practitioner (5)

DOWN

1 Point of entry (6)
2 Material from tusks (5)
3 Weeps noisily (4)
5 Church musician? (8)
6 Loud and harsh (7)
7 Staggered (6)
8 Throng (5)
13 Resounding (8)
15 Month (7)
17 Mighty, powerful (6)
18 Sea (5)
19 Bad temper (6)
22 Unreliable (5)
23 Horse for breeding (4)

ACROSS

1 Lady's maid (7)
5 Tempest (5)
8 Criminal (5)
9 Welsh mountain (7)
10 Hex look (4,3)
11 Strap (anag.) (5)
12 Soundless (6)
14 The East (6)
17 Sound made by a pig (5)
19 Sibling (7)
22 Came in (7)
23 Rigid (5)
24 Theatre seat (5)
25 Roads (7)

DOWN

1 Michael Caine film (5)
2 Hostility (3-4)
3 —— *Get Your Gun* (5)
4 Went over to one side (6)
5 Bung (7)
6 Command (5)
7 Send Tim (anag.) (7)
12 Small seals (7)
13 Inherent (7)
15 Intensify (7)
16 Tolerates (6)
18 Excessive(ly) (prefix) (5)
20 External (5)
21 Staggers (5)

100

ACROSS

1 Surplus (5)
5 Hot dish (5)
8 Hue (US spelling) (5)
9 Pigtail (5)
10 Beginning (9)
11 Hawaiian wreath (3)
12 The clarinet (anag.) (5,6)
15 Type of bus halting-place (7,4)
19 Flying saucer (3)
20 Serialised programme (4,5)
22 Whinny (5)
23 Cake covering (5)
24 Wood nymph (5)
25 Evict (5)

DOWN

1 Lattice-work (8)
2 Disastrous (6)
3 Set in motion (8)
4 Scent-bottle (6)
5 Harvest (4)
6 Widow (6)
7 Open mouth wide (4)
13 Sergeant (anag.) (8)
14 Glancing rebound (8)
16 Prey (6)
17 Dissertation (6)
18 Volcanic rock (6)
20 Slide (4)
21 Roman poet (4)

ACROSS

1 Irregular (5)
4 Vast ages (5)
10 Most affluent (7)
11 Change (5)
12 Caterpillar (5)
13 Finished work (7)
15 Moist (4)
17 Water-vapour (5)
19 Bird of prey (5)
22 Mope (anag.) (4)
25 Objection (7)
27 Layabout (5)
29 Proportion (5)
30 Hug (7)
31 Class; command (5)
32 Cut (5)

DOWN

2 Happen (5)
3 Caribbean island (7)
5 Precise (5)
6 Inborn (7)
7 Question; cook (5)
8 Tempest (5)
9 Unrefined (5)
14 Fencing sword (4)
16 Units of current (4)
18 Pig's foot (7)
20 Kindly (7)
21 Repudiate (5)
23 Aquatic mammal (5)
24 Avarice (5)
26 Wear down (5)
28 Depart (5)

102

ACROSS

1 Walker (5)
4 Staffed (6)
9 Turned aside (7)
10 Hatred (5)
11 Brood (4)
12 Groomed beauty (7)
13 Reverence (3)
14 Caustic (4)
16 Den (4)
18 Owed (3)
20 Not knowing (7)
21 Overabundance (4)
24 Staple (5)
25 Deal illegally (7)
26 Mock (6)
27 Vile (5)

DOWN

1 Husky (6)
2 Genuflect (5)
3 Ceremony (4)
5 Loveable (8)
6 Capital of Kenya (7)
7 Coy (6)
8 Maxim (5)
13 Progressed (8)
15 A scorer (anag.) (7)
17 Restricted (6)
18 Profundity (5)
19 Glutinous (6)
22 Raises (5)
23 Young deer (4)

ACROSS

1 Small mark (5)
4 Potato (colloq.) (5)
10 Overcome (7)
11 Distant planet (5)
12 George Cross island (5)
13 VIP (7)
15 Quantity of medicine (4)
17 Early Central American (5)
19 Pandit —— (5)
22 Conceal (4)
25 Rodent kept as pet (7)
27 Updated record (5)
29 Riddle (5)
30 Necessary (7)
31 eg Thrushes (5)
32 Dry stalks (5)

DOWN

2 Interviewing group (5)
3 Campaign (7)
5 —— and Omega (5)
6 South American state (7)
7 Rascal (5)
8 Residue (5)
9 Humorist (5)
14 Tear (4)
16 Darts line (4)
18 African river (7)
20 Most weird (7)
21 Spectre (5)
23 Incongruity (5)
24 Banishment (5)
26 Harris —— (5)
28 Criminal society (5)

104

ACROSS

5 Old French money (5)
8 German-born physicist (8)
9 Arbitrator (5)
10 Sufficient (8)
11 Social function (5)
14 Unity (3)
16 Section of poem (6)
17 Local regulations (6)
18 Small watch pocket (3)
20 Chirp (5)
24 Something extra in food (8)
25 Rush suddenly (5)
26 Punctilious person (8)
27 Heat-resistant glass (5)

DOWN

1 Award for distinction (5)
2 Beginning (5)
3 Dark beer (5)
4 Young cat (6)
6 Not throw-away (8)
7 One working late (5-3)
12 One hiding aboard (8)
13 Letter-container (8)
14 Lout (3)
15 Flow back (3)
19 Strange thing (6)
21 Snag (5)
22 Country house (5)
23 Cheerful (5)

ANSWERS

1

Across

1 Button
4 Whole
8 Ozone
9 Refused
10 Suggest
11 Anon
12 Hug
14 Stye
15 Rest
18 Dee
21 Arms
23 Blessed
25 Include
26 Orang
27 Slang
28 Lean-to

Down

1 Blouse
2 Thought
3 Open-eyed
4 Wife
5 Orson
6 Ending
7 Truth
13 Gruesome
16 Sustain
17 Matins
19 Ebbed
20 Adagio
22 Mecca
24 Rung

2

Across

1 Menuhin
8 French
9 Service
11 Anarchic
12 Again
14 Well
15 Bactrian
17 Scarcity
18 Bear
20 Daddy
21 Rare bird
23 Earlier
24 Cosset
25 Testate

Down

2 Emerge
3 Unveil
4 Inca
5 Pro rata
6 Unchained
7 Chicanery
10 Enrapture
12 Awestruck
13 Albatross
16 Scabies
18 Ballet
19 Advent
22 Dame

3

Across

1 Roc
3 Urn
5 Role
7 Vying
8 Damage
10 Lope
11 Plankton
13 Thread
14 Feeble
17 Optimist
19 Flaw
21 Fairer
22 Hindi
23 Clod
24 Yew
25 Eye

Down

1 Revolution
2 Clipper
3 Urge
4 Noddle
5 Reminder
6 Light
9 Underwrite
12 Hammered
15 Balance
16 Astray
18 Trawl
20 Show

4

Across
1 Borne
4 Apart
10 Altered
11 Admit
12 Opera
13 General
15 Teem
17 Liken
19 Inter
22 Date
25 Release
27 Actor
29 Swine
30 Oneness
31 Blade
32 Study

Down
2 Outré
3 Narrate
5 Prawn
6 Remorse
7 Sabot
8 Adage
9 Atoll
14 Emit
16 Ends
18 Ill-will
20 Nearest
21 Erase
23 Aesop
24 Press
26 Ahead
28 Tread

5

Across
1 Mass
4 Turkey
7 Use
9 Chop
10 Admitted
11 Ram
12 Mere
13 Sentries
16 Determination
19 Weakness
23 Dumb
24 Tap
25 Stranger
26 Owns
27 Ill
28 Make-up
29 Ease

Down
2 Achievements
3 Supreme
4 Teams
5 Roman
6 Enter
8 Developments
14 Exits
15 Tea
17 Ran
18 Tadpole
20 Koala
21 Eagle
22 Strip

6

Across
1 Proper
4 Gander
7 Pedagogue
9 Parr
10 Spit
11 Corgi
13 Ration
14 Edison
15 Nutmeg
17 Bogotá
19 Trait
20 Cope
22 Fail
23 Ephemeral
24 Rescue
25 Sprite

Down
1 Pauper
2 Peer
3 Reason
4 George
5 Nous
6 Rotten
7 Prototype
8 Episcopal
11 Comet
12 Idiot
15 Nectar
16 Greene
17 Biceps
18 Allure
21 Epic
22 Fair

7

Across
1 Grass
4 Routes
9 Eminent
10 Untie
11 Seek
12 Grecian
13 Ode
14 Tutu
16 Cage
18 Axe
20 Creased
21 Ibex
24 Undid
25 Proceed
26 Endure
27 Sites

Down
1 Grease
2 Alice
3 Step
5 Opulence
6 Totting
7 Skeins
8 Stage
13 Outsider
15 Up-ended
17 Accuse
18 Adept
19 Exodus
22 Bleat
23 Toss

8

Across
1 Tresco
4 Thick
8 Alias
9 Markets
10 Peering
11 Stye
12 End
14 Stag
15 Rule
18 Sir
21 Bail
23 Umpired
25 Says you
26 Inlet
27 Delos
28 Uglier

Down
1 Tramps
2 Evident
3 Castings
4 Tyro
5 Inert
6 Kisser
7 Image
13 Dropping
16 Lorelei
17 Abused
19 Run up
20 Editor
22 Idyll
24 Byes

9

Across
1 Battles
5 Card
7 Elgar
8 Column
10 Door
11 Eldorado
13 Retort
14 Lessee
17 Marathon
19 Hush
21 Hit out
22 Doing
23 Self
24 Dresden

Down
1 Breadcrumb
2 Tugboat
3 Lark
4 Sickle
5 Culloden
6 Rumba
9 Copenhagen
12 Write off
15 Studied
16 Booted
18 Rhine
20 Adze

10

Across
1 Beau
5 Ling
7 Steeple
8 Eyesight
10 Sort
12 Damp
14 Astonish
16 Ancestor
17 Dill
18 Idle
19 Declared
22 Certain
23 Huge
24 Twig

Down
1 Brie
2 Uses
3 Sergeant
4 Spot
5 Lessened
6 Gift
9 Yearned
11 Resolve
13 Pretence
15 Turncoat
18 Itch
19 Dark
20 Aunt
21 Drag

11

Across
7 Hissed
8 Oracle
10 Release
11 Queue
12 Shed
13 Grief
17 Brass
18 Kilo
22 Needs
23 Mistral
24 Enzyme
25 Vassal

Down
1 Cherish
2 Psalter
3 He-man
4 Croquet
5 Octet
6 Jewel
9 Wearisome
14 Presume
15 Diarist
16 Worldly
19 Annex
20 Seize
21 Essay

12

Across
1 Whacks
4 Paper
8 Rabid
9 Ailment
10 Lambeth
11 Inro
12 ABC
14 Knee
15 Hock
18 Era
21 Agog
23 Bequest
25 Clipped
26 Eliza
27 Nerve
28 Assent

Down
1 Warble
2 Albumen
3 Kedgeree
4 Pall
5 Paean
6 Ration
7 Dacha
13 Chequers
16 Crevice
17 Falcon
19 Abide
20 Stuart
22 Osier
24 Apse

13

 1 Ponchos
 5 Pilot
 8 Anger
 9 Resumes
 10 Testified
 12 Nil
 13 Comedy
 14 Stasis
 17 Ill
 18 Brown Bess
 20 Buttons
 21 Evade
 23 Ranch
 24 Literal

Down
 1 Plant
 2 Nag
 3 Hurried
 4 Sprain
 5 Posed
 6 Luminesce
 7 Tussles
 11 Simpleton
 13 Climber
 15 Tangent
 16 Fossil
 18 Booth
 19 Shell
 22 Air

14

Across
 1 Amman
 4 Feral
 10 Seasons
 11 Henry
 12 Haydn
 13 Airmail
 15 Ears
 17 Heidi
 19 Irish
 22 Rose
 25 Protest
 27 Tiger
 29 Carat
 30 Evident
 31 Appal
 32 Islay

Down
 2 Meaty
 3 Adorned
 5 Ether
 6 Annuals
 7 As the
 8 Oscar
 9 Cycle
 14 Isis
 16 Airs
 18 Ego-trip
 20 Retails
 21 Speck
 23 Other
 24 Broth
 26 Extra
 28 Greta

15

Across
 1 Valley
 7 Diction
 8 Unbutton
 9 Attic
 10 Hyena
 11 Taxi
 12 Icing
 15 Alias
 16 Grill
 19 Alga
 20 Cling
 21 Nervy
 22 Orangery
 23 Subside
 24 Blithe

Down
 1 Vouching
 2 Libretti
 3 Extra
 4 Win
 5 Static
 6 Lotion
 7 Doctrinaire
 9 Axis
 13 Imminent
 14 Gargoyle
 15 Ally
 17 Rhesus
 18 Lavish
 20 Canal
 22 Odd

16

Across

1 Write
4 Sighed
9 Lasagne
10 Often
11 Used
12 Loathes
13 Set
14 Abet
16 Rota
18 Lay
20 Trounce
21 Race
24 Tetra
25 Soldier
26 Deride
27 Taste

Down

1 Walrus
2 Issue
3 Edge
5 Idolatry
6 Hatchet
7 Dynast
8 Dealt
13 Standard
15 Bloater
17 Stated
18 Least
19 Decree
22 Aries
23 Flat

17

Across

1 Beak
4 Hoarse
7 Ire
9 Odin
10 Awakened
11 Gel
12 Bald
13 Sentries
16 Commemoration
19 Precedes
23 Dumb
24 Cap
25 Inferior
26 Owns
27 Ail
28 Esteem
29 Ease

Down

2 Endeavouring
3 Kingdom
4 Heals
5 Again
6 Sheer
8 Developments
14 Erode
15 Tea
17 Ewe
18 Tadpole
20 Chess
21 Drive
22 Scram

18

Across

1 River
4 Tigress
8 Miracle
9 Lotus
10 Aloft
11 Logical
13 Teem
15 Thorax
17 Evaded
20 Iona
22 Memento
24 Robot
26 Lists
27 Laid off
28 Results
29 Hotel

Down

1 Rampant
2 Virgo
3 Ricotta
4 Treble
5 Gulag
6 Enticed
7 Sisal
12 Omen
14 Exit
16 Osmosis
18 Varnish
19 Dutiful
21 Oodles
22 Molar
23 Nasal
25 Boost

19

Across

1 Pancake
5 Raise
8 Later
9 Ballads
10 Tubular
11 Aryan
12 Breton
14 Strike
17 Rowed
19 Skillet
22 Mancini
23 Crime
24 Nodal
25 Insults

Down

1 Pilot
2 Notable
3 April
4 Embark
5 Reliant
6 Italy
7 Essence
12 Birdman
13 Old bill
15 Ill-will
16 Assisi
18 Waned
20 Incas
21 Trees

20

Across

4 Auntie
7 Aircraft
8 Signal
10 Stamina
11 Blue
13 Festival
14 Pray
16 User
18 Rendered
19 Isle
21 Mithras
22 Athens
24 Engineer
25 Errata

Down

1 Distress
2 Scimitars
3 Carnivore
4 ATS
5 Tender
6 Eulogy
9 Ill
11 Blandings
12 Upper-hand
15 Averages
16 Unsafe
17 Either
20 Len
23 Sea

21

Across

1 Welling
5 Tonne
8 Amass
9 Noticed
10 Exonerate
12 See
13 Decade
14 Harass
17 Ode
18 Hackneyed
20 Potable
21 Scorn
23 Dealt
24 Meander

Down

1 Whale
2 Lea
3 Instead
4 Genial
5 Title
6 Necessary
7 Endless
11 Orchestra
13 Dropped
15 Amnesia
16 Scream
18 Habit
19 Donor
22 Odd

22

Across
1 Creek
4 Heaters
8 Use
9 Too
10 Image
11 Pitch
12 Engaged
15 Else
17 Throne
19 Auntie
22 Sort
24 Biggest
26 Topic
28 Stand
30 Ear
31 Pip
32 Decides
33 Yarns

Down
1 Crumpet
2 Event
3 Kitchen
4 Hooves
5 Aping
6 Era
7 Spend
13 Near
14 Gut
16 Less
18 Rag
20 Utterly
21 Escapes
23 Others
24 Based
25 Ended
27 Paper
29 Arc

23

Across
1 Granary
5 Bred
7 Exalt
8 Arcane
10 Tidy
11 Flashing
13 Canine
14 Beggar
17 Teenager
19 Derv
21 Aurora
22 Duvet
23 Plus
24 Misused

Down
1 Great Scott
2 Abandon
3 Acts
4 Yearly
5 Buckshee
6 Ennui
9 Aggravated
12 Infamous
15 Greaves
16 Becalm
18 Equal
20 Odds

24

Across
1 Axe
3 Sea
5 Dent
7 Gypsy
8 Garage
10 Esau
11 Electron
13 Tangle
14 See 17
17 & 14 Nine
    Men's Morris
19 Zulu
21 Nature
22 Which
23 Half
24 Tin
25 Gas

Down
1 Augmenting
2 Explain
3 Says
4 Argyll
5 Director
6 Niger
9 Inasmuch as
12 Plum duff
15 Rousing
16 Intent
18 Nyasa
20 Twin

25

Across

1 Two parts
5 Mild
8 Embitter
9 Diet
11 Deformation
14 Alp
16 Erred
17 Let
18 Horizontals
21 Slim
22 Mandible
24 Oust
25 Born Free

Down

1 Tree
2 Orbed
3 Antifreeze
4 Tie
6 Initial
7 Detonate
10 Handmaiden
12 Rerun
13 Machismo
15 Porkies
19 Sober
20 Pele
23 Ado

26

Across

1 Arrow
4 Gait
8 Compass
9 Coved
10 Tenon
11 Observe
13 Petite
15 Sluice
17 Leakage
20 Usher
22 Cocoa
23 Algebra
24 Skit
25 Degum

Down

1 Ascot
2 Remonstrance
3 Whatnot
4 Gusto
5 Incus
6 Overnight bag
7 Adhere
12 Bus
13 Policy
14 Egg
16 Lounged
18 Aback
19 Exact
21 Realm

27

Across

1 Knotting
7 Thyme
8 Appetiser
9 New
10 Easy
11 Flying
13 Pedant
14 Reward
17 Screen
18 Best
20 Fit
22 Segregate
23 Crass
24 Gradient

Down

1 Knave
2 Opposed
3 Tots
4 Nestle
5 Lying
6 Seaweed
7 Trainer
12 Ingress
13 Perfect
15 Average
16 Beggar
17 Steal
19 Tweet
21 Read

28

Across
1 Diner
4 Might
10 Coastal
11 Draws
12 Preen
13 Realise
15 Data
17 Dress
19 Sings
22 Keen
25 Compass
27 Jetty
29 Nurse
30 Arrange
31 Aside
32 Adorn

Down
2 Image
3 Extends
5 India
6 Heading
7 Scope
8 Alert
9 Osier
14 Ease
16 Asks
18 Remarks
20 Injured
21 Scene
23 Essay
24 Bytes
26 Amend
28 Tenor

29

Across
1 Whale
4 Beaune
9 Corsets
10 Badge
11 Ella
12 Ordered
13 Tun
14 Yo-yo
16 Eros
18 Mad
20 Croatia
21 Over
24 Truro
25 Gorilla
26 Eldest
27 Moans

Down
1 Wicker
2 April
3 Even
5 Embedded
6 Undergo
7 Emends
8 & 22 Aston Villa
13 Tortuous
15 Orotund
17 Scythe
18 Madge
19 Broads
22 See 8
23 Brum

30

Across
1 Giver
3 Kidder
7 Camcorder
9 This
10 Week
11 Pleas
13 Surely
14 Nomad
15 Count
17 Coarse
20 Kudos
21 Lois
23 Heat
24 Scrunched
25 Beat it
26 Spend

Down
1 Gratis
2 Eras
3 Korean
4 Drew
5 Ranks
6 Scaly
7 Cirrhosis
8 Remarried
11 Plonk
12 Solos
16 Tumult
17 Conch
18 Extend
19 Climb
22 Scat
23 Help

31

Across
1 Minimise
5 Zing
8 Come down
9 Hell
11 Deliberated
14 Hag
16 Surge
17 Apt
18 Acrimonious
21 Aged
22 Aviatrix
24 Ta-ta
25 Fallible

Down
1 Muck
2 Nomad
3 Meddlesome
4 Saw
6 Inertia
7 Gelidity
10 Free-for-all
12 Baron
13 Pheasant
15 Garment
19 Scrub
20 Axle
23 Via

32

Across
1 Broker
4 Knout
8 Swing
9 Elevate
10 Omitted
11 West
12 Inn
14 Mere
15 Ever
18 Nap
21 Only
23 Imagine
25 Compact
26 Ideal
27 Ratio
28 Snatch

Down
1 Bishop
2 Orifice
3 Eighteen
4 Keep
5 Ovate
6 Twenty
7 Verdi
13 Negation
16 Eminent
17 Concur
19 Piste
20 Health
22 Limit
24 Halo

33

Across
1 Severn
4 Seize
8 Rumba
9 Pleased
10 Painter
11 Bede
12 Kos
14 Ages
15 Puff
18 Tip
21 Ripe
23 & 28 Airs and graces
25 Canvass
26 Lotto
27 Ducks
28 See 23

Down
1 Scraps
2 Vamping
3 Road-test
4 Stem
5 Issue
6 Eddies
7 Spark
13 Sparkler
16 Frantic
17 Traced
19 Pansy
20 Odious
22 Panic
24 Pass

34

Across
1 Cote
4 Hangars
8 Stalwart
9 Pal
11 Acetic
13 Arrant
14 Ritzy
15 Kick
17 Rent
18 Metro
20 Amulet
21 Eskimo
24 Met
25 Gardenia
26 Nursery
27 Deaf

Down
2 Outré
3 Éclair
4 Hoax
5 Notary
6 Appease
7 Salutation
10 Backgammon
12 Civet
13 Azure
16 Counter
18 Meagre
19 Ostend
22 Ibiza
23 Fray

35

Across
1 Suite
4 Dreams
9 Curious
10 Peter
11 Esse
12 Emotion
13 Cur
14 Zero
16 Eels
18 Bad
20 Perjury
21 Gozo
24 Regan
25 Andiron
26 Orders
27 Ether

Down
1 Soccer
2 Idris
3 Eton
5 Reproved
6 Ant-hill
7 Sarong
8 Aster
13 Columnar
15 Enraged
17 Oporto
18 Bylaw
19 Corner
22 Oprah
23 Edge

36

Across
1 Know
4 Ozark
8 Two by two
9 Ibis
10 Eddy
11 Operates
12 Intact
14 Ararat
16 Reindeer
19 Iris
20 Flea
21 Contours
22 Basil
23 Else

Down
2 Nobly
3 Without
4 Ozone
5 Ali Baba
6 Knife
7 Sweden
13 Annuals
14 Arrange
15 Apiary
17 Ex lib
18 Excel
19 Idols

37

Across

4 Nippon
5 Tuck
7 Sinuous
10 Waist
11 Mullein
12 Screw
14 Private
15 Opera
16 Onerous
20 Chalk
21 Yule-log
22 Tong
23 Perish

Down

1 Opium
2 Mogul
3 Durance
4 Naïf
6 Kismet
8 Outrank
9 Slavery
10 Wistful
13 Upshot
14 Prolong
17 Outer
18 Sepia
19 Both

38

Across

7 League
8 Allies
10 Convene
11 Amaze
12 Idea
13 Given
17 Camel
18 Male
22 Light
23 Curtail
24 Ballot
25 Retain

Down

1 Flaccid
2 Painter
3 Quiet
4 Pleaded
5 Rival
6 Ashen
9 Residence
14 Caption
15 Caravan
16 Decline
19 Globe
20 Agile
21 Brief

39

Across

1 Solace
7 Hitters
8 Complain
9 Utter
10 Nears
11 Else
12 Edges
15 Liner
16 Scene
19 East
20 Reeds
21 Break
22 Anything
23 Peeling
24 Boughs

Down

1 Sickness
2 Lambaste
3 Calls
4 Sin
5 Stated
6 Breeze
7 Hibernating
9 User
13 Greeting
14 Sausages
15 Leak
17 Cornea
18 Neatly
20 Ratio
22 Ant

40

Across
1 Handy
4 Capped
9 Denmark
10 Means
11 Rise
12 Lineage
13 Awl
14 Well
16 Slew
18 Doh
20 Reverse
21 Jazz
24 Proms
25 Apparel
26 Despot
27 Tonga

Down
1 Hedera
2 Nones
3 Year
5 Admonish
6 Placate
7 Disney
8 Skull
13 Alfresco
15 Envious
17 Griped
18 Degas
19 Azalea
22 Aaron
23 Spat

41

Across
1 Palin
4 Inter
10 Resting
11 Notch
12 Admit
13 Intrude
15 Iona
17 Touch
19 Voter
22 Item
25 Visitor
27 Imply
29 Ivory
30 Propane
31 Aside
32 Using

Down
2 Assam
3 Idiotic
5 Nonet
6 Extrude
7 Cream
8 Again
9 Chief
14 Nave
16 Ohio
18 Osseous
20 Ominous
21 Avoid
23 Trips
24 Pyres
26 Toyed
28 Plain

42

Across
1 Cruz
4 Control
8 Emitting
9 Sag
11 Quaver
13 Old hat
14 Rinse
15 Etch
17 Spam
18 Seven
20 Zanier
21 Rabbit
24 Boo
25 Tenerife
26 Ximenes
27 Wage

Down
2 Rumba
3 Zither
4 Chin
5 Niggle
6 Rosehip
7 Legitimate
10 Squeeze-box
12 River
13 Osier
16 Conform
18 Sexton
19 Narrow
22 Befog
23 Onus

43

Across
1 Wren
5 Yule
7 Awesome
8 Pole star
10 Ripe
12 Mild
14 Examined
16 Disaster
17 Gain
18 Snug
19 Bandages
22 Triumph
23 Mass
24 Ever

Down
1 Wasp
2 Name
3 Sentient
4 Boar
5 Yearning
6 Edge
9 Opinion
11 Precise
13 Draughts
15 Agronomy
18 Slim
19 Brie
20 Ache
21 Stir

44

Across
1 Paris
4 Heights
8 Moa
9 Run
10 Dingo
11 Extra
12 Snarled
15 Mate
17 Stress
19 Turtle
22 Kiss
24 Sadness
26 Exits
28 Order
30 Use
31 Axe
32 Ponchos
33 Stern

Down
1 Pampers
2 React
3 Screams
4 Honest
5 India
6 Hen
7 Stood
13 Nets
14 Let
16 Asks
18 Red
20 Useless
21 Eastern
23 Issues
24 Stoop
25 Earth
27 Image
29 Din

45

Across
1 Brick
4 Stun
7 Pass
8 Oratorio
9 Humankind
10 Rex
12 Rancid
14 Deride
16 Quo
18 Gladstone
21 Junk mail
22 Rude
23 Zany
24 Train

Down
1 Bravura
2 Instance
3 Knock
4 Slow
5 Unite
6 Warned
11 Criteria
13 Dollar
15 Dunedin
17 Uvula
19 Delft
20 Okay

46

Across
1 Incur
4 Wrecked
8 Sharpen
9 Panic
10 Aggro
11 Literal
13 Open
15 Typify
17 Fender
20 Root
22 Harrier
24 Cream
26 Nosed
27 Evident
28 Holdall
29 Gulch

Down
1 Instant
2 Clang
3 Reproof
4 Winkle
5 Expat
6 Kindred
7 Ducal
12 Info
14 Pyre
16 Parasol
18 Etching
19 Rematch
21 Ordeal
22 Hunch
23 India
25 Ewell

47

Across
1 La Belle
5 Dame
7 Songs
8 Mersey
10 Nile
11 Unitised
13 Ensure
14 Mobile
17 Eviction
19 Poet
21 Sonnet
22 Keats
23 Dyke
24 Nemesis

Down
1 Los Angeles
2 Bangles
3 Lust
4 Ermine
5 Duration
6 Meets
9 Advertises
12 Pretence
15 Isobars
16 Boston
18 Ivory
20 Skim

48

Across
1 Tolkien
5 Enya
7 Sleep
8 Church
10 Moor
11 Maharaja
13 Sonata
14 Helped
17 Elliptic
19 Stye
21 Psyche
22 Rheum
23 Zeal
24 Slumber

Down
1 Taskmaster
2 Lie down
3 Impi
4 Nectar
5 Emulated
6 Yucca
9 Daydreamer
12 Atypical
15 Pot-herb
16 Biceps
18 Lisle
20 Frau

49

Across
1 Siren
4 Sister
9 Upstart
10 Steer
11 Goya
12 Reliant
13 Boy
14 Late
16 Need
18 Apt
20 Reading
21 Stye
24 Grain
25 Instant
26 Entire
27 Yield

Down
1 Smudge
2 Risky
3 Neat
5 Insolent
6 Teenage
7 Rarity
8 Story
13 Beginner
15 Adamant
17 Brogue
18 Again
19 Heated
22 Trace
23 Espy

50

Across
5 Falls
8 Pretence
9 Scare
10 Leverets
11 Spoon
14 Ere
16 Petrol
17 Steers
18 Ilk
20 Cluck
24 Murderer
25 Topol
26 Chairman
27 Stash

Down
1 Apple
2 Serve
3 Weary
4 Scoter
6 Accepted
7 Larboard
12 Sells out
13 Gracious
14 Eli
15 Esk
19 Laughs
21 Oddie
22 Crumb
23 Crane

51

Across
1 Tonies
7 Cronies
8 Ambrosia
9 Argot
10 Query
11 Rita
12 Okays
15 Aesop
16 Lunar
19 Liar
20 Queer
21 Bread
22 Pinafore
23 Jackpot
24 Sleepy

Down
1 Tranquil
2 Nobleman
3 Ebony
4 Era
5 Anorak
6 Felony
7 Citrus fruit
9 Atop
13 Antelope
14 Scarcely
15 Arid
17 Uproar
18 Alaska
20 Quail
22 Pot

52

Across
1 Why
3 Doe
5 Penn
7 Impel
8 Tobago
10 Prim
11 Artistic
13 Rigour
14 Hawaii
17 Nominate
19 Pant
21 Tivoli
22 Mayor
23 Seat
24 Eat
25 Ess

Down
1 Whispering
2 Yapping
3 Dole
4 Extort
5 Publican
6 Night
9 Scriptures
12 Burnt out
15 Analyse
16 Stride
18 Maize
20 Emit

53

Across
1 Pore
4 House
8 Twitcher
9 Seen
10 Alto
11 Conclude
12 Dermal
14 Bungle
16 Classics
19 Gibe
20 Lima
21 Inimical
22 Eland
23 Gulf

Down
2 Outdo
3 Ethical
4 Heron
5 Upsilon
6 Emend
7 Twelve
13 Mascara
14 Basking
15 Libyan
17 Loire
18 Iliad
19 Grill

54

Across
1 Knows
5 Dives
8 Whale
9 Alibi
10 Monologue
11 Sal
12 Equidistant
15 Kleptomania
19 Bop
20 Registrar
22 Oscar
23 Adieu
24 Fry-up
25 Sisal

Down
1 Knapsack
2 Oriole
3 Swimsuit
4 Canned
5 Dell
6 Viagra
7 Side
13 Sonorous
14 Temporal
16 Eighty
17 Martin
18 Abacus
20 Reef
21 Soap

55

Across
1 Stony
4 Baroque
8 Concern
9 Omagh
10 Emend
11 Arbiter
13 Etna
15 Deride
17 Carrot
20 Aped
22 Deplore
24 Haste
26 Edict
27 Narrows
28 Stand-in
29 Demon

Down
1 Succeed
2 Ounce
3 Yielded
4 Bunyan
5 Rhomb
6 Quarter
7 Ether
12 Race
14 Tear
16 Replica
18 Adhered
19 Treason
21 Pennon
22 Deeds
23 Opted
25 Storm

56

Across
1 Follow
4 Vaunts
7 Cassettes
9 Mood
10 Scar
11 Tears
13 Litres
14 Sagest
15 Alarms
17 Permit
19 Sates
20 Cuts
22 Knew
23 Supposing
24 Tissue
25 Needed

Down
1 Formal
2 Load
3 Wishes
4 Voters
5 Uses
6 Secret
7 Contrasts
8 Screaming
11 Terms
12 Saves
15 Accent
16 Sample
17 Person
18 Toward
21 Sues
22 Knee

57

Across
1 Stephen
8 Buyers
9 Baggage
11 Oxbridge
12 Feuds
14 Ella
15 Misspent
17 Upstarts
18 Etna
20 Easel
21 Deadwood
23 Neutral
24 Treble
25 Starter

Down
2 Teasel
3 Pagoda
4 Ergo
5 Bulrush
6 Deadbeats
7 Essential
10 Expiation
12 Fecundity
13 Ullswater
16 Jaywalk
18 Easter
19 Negate
22 Deft

58

Across
1 Hare
4 Raisin
7 Nae
9 & 29 As it were
10 Monotone
11 Roi
12 Isle
13 Tartaric
16 Distinguished
19 Mariners
23 Airy
24 Ail
25 Temporal
26 Love
27 Ago
28 Glared
29 See 9

Down
2 Assassinated
3 Entreat
4 Remit
5 Inner
6 Intra
8 Engine driver
14 Anger
15 Tai
17 Inn
18 Swallow
20 Impel
21 Error
22 Salad

59

Across
1 Booby
4 Prise
10 Schools
11 Dunce
12 Earth
13 Aerials
15 Emma
17 Zorro
19 Swish
22 Bath
25 Goldwyn
27 Index
29 Owned
30 Replies
31 Gofer
32 Broke

Down
2 Other
3 Brother
5 Rider
6 Sundays
7 Usher
8 Islam
9 Tease
14 East
16 Moby
18 Orlando
20 Whisper
21 Egg on
23 Angry
24 Exist
26 Wedge
28 Drink

60

Across
1 Ding
5 Dong
7 Merrily
8 Furnaced
10 Sock
12 Scan
14 Iniquity
16 Overshoe
17 Faze
18 Clio
19 Exponent
22 Eyebrow
23 Ajar
24 They

Down
1 Duff
2 G-man
3 Brackish
4 Wind
5 Dyestuff
6 Gunk
9 Uncivil
11 Citizen
13 Narrower
15 Inexpert
18 Coma
19 Ewer
20 Nowt
21 Tiny

61

Across
1 Stocked
8 Aching
9 En masse
11 Exterior
12 Aesop
14 Bran
15 Becoming
17 Idealist
18 Blot
20 Grebe
21 Abortive
23 Excited
24 Easily
25 Immense

Down
2 Tender
3 Crayon
4 Erse
5 Echelon
6 Divisible
7 Aggregate
10 Expensive
12 Abdicated
13 Safe house
16 All told
18 Bruise
19 Obsess
22 Exam

62

Across
1 Allot
4 Omani
10 Haggard
11 Noise
12 Putti
13 Porthos
15 Oath
17 Brunt
19 Inure
22 Oboe
25 Lissome
27 Amble
29 Named
30 Re-elect
31 Adore
32 Aside

Down
2 Light
3 Oration
5 Minor
6 Neither
7 Chops
8 Adept
9 Messy
14 Ohio
16 Atom
18 Resumed
20 Neatens
21 Blind
23 Berry
24 Teeth
26 Order
28 Bread

63

Across
1 Goal
4 De luxe
7 Oar
9 Stet
10 Escargot
11 Tea
12 Ogle
13 Relaxing
16 Encyclopaedia
19 Treaties
23 Brew
24 Oil
25 Handicap
26 Eats
27 Pom
28 Sturdy
29 Sulk

Down
2 Octogenarian
3 Lottery
4 Drear
5 Local
6 Xerox
8 Coincidental
14 Erode
15 Aga
17 Cot
18 Emblems
20 Audit
21 Incur
22 Soppy

64

Across
1 Plains
4 Potter
7 Disappear
9 Rues
10 Keen
11 Screw
13 Depute
14 Tidier
15 Apiary
17 Atkins
19 Early
20 View
22 Snub
23 Downright
24 Tended
25 Sadist

Down
1 Putrid
2 Iris
3 Scarce
4 Puppet
5 Teak
6 Runner
7 Despaired
8 Recipient
11 Stare
12 Witty
15 Advent
16 Yawned
17 Allies
18 Submit
21 Wood
22 Shed

65

Across
1 Miss
5 Elle
7 Heinous
8 Browbeat
10 Over
12 Spot
14 Treasure
16 Reminder
17 Sure
18 Psst
19 Pastrami
22 Cantata
23 Posh
24 Real

Down
1 Moab
2 Show
3 Directed
4 Most
5 Espouses
6 Ever
9 Repress
11 Eardrum
13 Triptych
15 Etruscan
18 Prop
19 Pony
20 Rear
21 Idol

66

Across
1 She
3 His
5 Moor
7 Tubby
8 Pitted
10 Than
11 Censured
13 Wrench
14 Pistol
17 Repaired
19 Cats
21 Humble
22 Adieu
23 Edge
24 Sot
25 Gas

Down
1 Sets to work
2 Embrace
3 Hwyl
4 Septet
5 Mateship
6 One-er
9 Odalisques
12 Scribble
15 Teasing
16 Severs
18 Pound
20 Haft

67

Across
1 North
4 Carole
9 Liner
10 Raleigh
11 Oration
12 Excel
14 Cud
15 & 16 Sky Lab
16 See 15
18 Sir
21 Audio
22 Triplet
23 Timpani
25 Lithe
26 Durham
27 Plead

Down
1 Nelson
2 Ransacked
3 Heroic
5 Allied
6 Obi
7 Exhale
8 Iron curtain
13 Charlotte
17 Ranted
18 Sonata
19 Fillip
20 Attend
24 Mar

68

Across
1 Passion
5 Flour
8 Avoid
9 Lambada
10 Simpson
11 Llama
12 Tangle
14 Assume
17 Tunic
19 Neutral
22 Extrude
23 Sight
24 Sidle
25 Estates

Down
1 Peaks
2 Snowman
3 Indus
4 Nylons
5 Fumbles
6 Omaha
7 Real ale
12 Totters
13 Lecture
15 Upright
16 Annexe
18 Noted
20 Upset
21 Laths

69

Across
1 Carry on
8 Neater
9 Channel
11 Romantic
12 Sleep
14 Tend
15 Launches
17 Economic
18 Once
20 Urged
21 Curtains
23 Sadness
24 Engine
25 Depends

Down
2 Awhile
3 Rented
4 Over
5 Remains
6 Stitching
7 Processed
10 Locations
12 Stretched
13 Encourage
16 Cocaine
18 Orange
19 Ceased
22 Save

70

Across
1 Mecca
4 Nicks
10 Incisor
11 Label
12 Opera
13 Assault
15 Rode
17 Gouda
19 Amaze
22 Tale
25 Delight
27 Aitch
29 Plans
30 Neutral
31 Ascot
32 Helot

Down
2 Emcee
3 Custard
5 Idles
6 Kibbutz
7 Bigot
8 Dread
9 Blitz
14 Seal
16 Oath
18 Orleans
20 Measure
21 Adept
23 Atone
24 Whelk
26 Gusto
28 Torso

71

Across
1 Sicker
4 Faint
8 Cross
9 Roofing
10 Embarks
11 Ogre
12 Hog
14 Grin
15 Ripe
18 Gun
21 Orgy
23 Implode
25 Tabasco
26 Ibiza
27 Ringo
28 Agreed

Down
1 Soccer
2 Clobber
3 Ensuring
4 Frog
5 Icing
6 Tagged
7 Brash
13 Gripping
16 Provide
17 Porter
19 Nixon
20 Gerald
22 Gabon
24 Oslo

72

Across
1 Chalet
7 Winters
8 Poseidon
9 Movie
10 Falla
11 Leek
12 Rebel
15 Rosie
16 Arena
19 Ever
20 Overt
21 Dance
22 Mescalin
23 Debates
24 Prayer

Down
1 Cup of tea
2 Absolute
3 Erica
4 Gin
5 Stroke
6 Praise
7 World series
9 Mere
13 Beverley
14 Listener
15 Rave
17 Reader
18 Nectar
20 Occur
22 Mel

73

Across
1 High
4 Queue
8 Dissolve
9 Peat
10 Gout
11 Wardroom
12 Bright
14 Brainy
16 Quotient
19 Fade
20 Thai
21 Camomile
22 Regal
23 Surf

Down
2 Inset
3 Halfwit
4 Queer
5 Emporia
6 Erato
7 Rigour
13 G-string
14 Betimes
15 Noddle
17 Usher
18 Excel
19 Femur

74

Across
1 Sec
3 Sly
5 Sand
7 Video
8 Taipei
10 Siva
11 Meddling
13 Orrery
14 Pedlar
17 Edgewise
19 Ages
21 Braise
22 Capri
23 Gong
24 Dun
25 Nun

Down
1 Saves money
2 Cadaver
3 Spot
4 Yatter
5 Swindled
6 Naevi
9 Aggression
12 Browning
15 Leg-spin
16 Ascend
18 Garbo
20 Scan

75

Across
1 Along
4 Weigh
10 Elastic
11 Tames
12 Lasso
13 Tangled
15 Need
17 Balsa
19 Abyss
22 Same
25 Recover
27 Drama
29 Spies
30 Stomach
31 Unite
32 Smelt

Down
2 Leans
3 Notions
5 Eaten
6 Gambles
7 Yells
8 Acute
9 Aside
14 Adam
16 Ease
18 Auction
20 Bedroom
21 Grasp
23 Arise
24 Yacht
26 Visit
28 Avail

76

Across
1 Handles
5 Largo
8 Lorry
9 Anguine
10 Ego-trip
11 Breed
12 Costly
14 Severe
17 Lemon
19 Obscene
22 Recluse
23 Drama
24 Tuned
25 Hatchet

Down
1 Halve
2 Nervous
3 Layer
4 Scampi
5 Legible
6 Rhine
7 Overdue
12 Culprit
13 Languid
15 Eye-wash
16 Joseph
18 Mâcon
20 Sadat
21 Exact

77

Across
1 Allyson
5 Wanda
8 Eland
9 Carroll
10 Atonement
12 Ivy
13 Repast
14 Lashed
17 Air
18 Empirical
20 Hounded
21 Nooks
23 Dread
24 Shelley

Down
1 Arena
2 Lea
3 Sadness
4 Nickel
5 Worst
6 Neolithic
7 Allayed
11 Opportune
13 Reached
15 Arrange
16 Spades
18 Ended
19 Lusty
22 Oil

78

Across
4 Lester
5 Jung
7 Charlie
10 Parka
11 Oil well
12 Alert
14 Fallacy
15 Rehab
16 Termite
20 Broad
21 Breaker
22 Ogle
23 Angler

Down
1 Astro
2 Peril
3 Aurally
4 Lahr
6 Go-kart
8 Lie-abed
9 Ewe-lamb
10 Placate
13 Weirdo
14 Fatally
17 Irony
18 Earls
19 Tear

79

Across
1 Mini
4 School
7 Nut
9 Stag
10 Unartful
11 Roc
12 Orca
13 Keystone
16 Penny-pinching
19 Eternity
23 Cowl
24 Opt
25 Lopsided
26 Arty
27 Ear
28 Entail
29 Euro

Down
2 Intersection
3 Ingrain
4 Stuck
5 Heavy
6 Octet
8 Running water
14 Evict
15 Sac
17 Yon
18 Hectare
20 Risen
21 India
22 Yodel

80

Across
1 Cause
4 Sting
10 Oceania
11 Ample
12 Snare
13 Rescued
15 Sled
17 Chase
19 Grief
22 Epee
25 Convoke
27 Strut
29 Fling
30 Carping
31 Agate
32 Jewel

Down
2 Arena
3 Sunless
5 Tears
6 Neptune
7 Moose
8 Nacre
9 Ready
14 Edge
16 Leek
18 Hanging
20 Reserve
21 Scoff
23 Peach
24 Stage
26 Ought
28 Raise

81

Across
1 Jolly
4 Boating
8 Whether
9 Opera
10 Omega
11 Options
13 Vote
15 Esteem
17 Suited
20 & 27 Eton College
22 Neptune
24 Rugby
26 Helps
27 See 20
28 Worktop
29 Dodos

Down
1 Jawbone
2 Liège
3 Yo-heave
4 Bardot
5 About
6 Iceboat
7 Grabs
12 Peso
14 Omen
16 Tippler
18 Unruled
19 Dryness
21 Teacup
22 Nohow
23 Upset
25 Greed

82

Across
1 Backed
4 Eerier
7 Bacterium
9 Lien
10 Till
11 Scent
13 Wicket
14 Tattoo
15 Armful
17 Fluent
19 Movie
20 Germ
22 Fort
23 Kerfuffle
24 Twitch
25 Legion

Down
1 Billow
2 Khan
3 Detect
4 Errant
5 Rout
6 Rialto
7 Benchmark
8 Mistletoe
11 Serum
12 Table
15 August
16 Loofah
17 Fitful
18 Titian
21 Melt
22 Flog

83

Across
1 Piquant
5 Chews
8 Apart
9 Run-down
10 Effects
11 Eject
12 Update
14 Ulster
17 Grave
19 Realist
22 Exhibit
23 Liken
24 Taste
25 Residue

Down
1 Place
2 Quaffed
3 Attic
4 Thrash
5 Conceal
6 Erode
7 Senator
12 Unguent
13 Tremble
15 Tricked
16 Orator
18 Aphis
20 Atlas
21 Tense

84

Across
1 Purse
4 Severe
9 Tractor
10 Sieve
11 Oath
12 Adamant
13 Dim
14 Fame
16 Iota
18 Arc
20 Complex
21 Calm
24 Apron
25 Oppress
26 Reside
27 Rites

Down
1 Python
2 Roast
3 Eats
5 Ecstatic
6 Elegant
7 Elects
8 Dream
13 Declined
15 Admires
17 Eclair
18 Axiom
19 Amuses
22 Alert
23 Spur

85

Across
1 Phew
4 Margate
8 Confused
9 Jet
11 Insult
13 Random
14 Errol
15 Tier
17 Bell
18 Ceres
20 Record
21 Rating
24 Oar
25 Adequate
26 Sitwell
27 Lure

Down
2 Hoops
3 Waffle
4 Mask
5 Radial
6 Adjudge
7 Entomology
10 Victorious
12 Tried
13 Rover
16 Excerpt
18 Create
19 Samuel
22 Inter
23 Zeal

86

Across
1 Anais
4 Capote
9 Ontario
10 Loins
11 Nice
12 Daytime
13 Ass
14 Fall
16 Nose
18 Nag
20 Marlene
21 Gala
24 Conga
25 Untried
26 Shekel
27 Piece

Down
1 Amount
2 Attic
3 Sore
5 Allaying
6 Origins
7 Ensues
8 Goods
13 Alienate
15 Arrange
17 Smacks
18 Nexus
19 Paddle
22 Arise
23 Stop

87

Across
1 Hove
4 Verdun
7 NCO
9 Acts
10 Lordship
11 Use
12 USSR
13 Scratchy
16 Good Queen
   Bess
19 Hand over
23 Smew
24 Ops
25 Alderney
26 Ouse
27 Coo
28 Adhere
29 Nosh

Down
2 Occasionally
3 Ensured
4 Voles
5 Rarer
6 Upset
8 Airhostesses
14 Crewe
15 Ann
17 Quo
18 Bassoon
20 Dread
21 Venue
22 Royce

88

Across
1 **& 5** Monte Carlo
8 Ruler
9 Adieu
10 Potential
11 Bye
12 Daisy-cutter
15 Litigiously
19 Eco
20 Racing car
22 Onset
23 Kapok
24 Horse
25 Egypt

Down
1 Meatball
2 Noised
3 Erupting
4 Glitzy
5 Cran
6 Resist
7 Oval
13 Upstroke
14 Rheostat
16 Ticker
17 Occupy
18 Yeasty
20 Ruth
21 Nuke

89

Across
1 Curter
4 Seize
8 Rifle
9 Operate
10 Marring
11 Mere
12 Hit
14 Mesh
15 Alto
18 Tow
21 Hide
23 Ageless
25 Romance
26 Taboo
27 Shrug
28 Adhere

Down
1 Chrome
2 Referee
3 Eyesight
4 Stew
5 Inane
6 Eleven
7 Bough
13 Talented
16 Tremble
17 Charts
19 Waver
20 Ashore
22 Demur
24 Snag

90

Across
1 Prophet
8 Tickle
9 Haulier
11 Repartee
12 Ember
14 User
15 Together
17 Outraged
18 Gnat
20 Eagle
21 Isolated
23 Dinners
24 Emends
25 Sawdust

Down
2 Realms
3 Pilfer
4 Ewer
5 Minaret
6 Sketching
7 Celebrate
10 Recovered
12 Eulogised
13 Beethoven
16 Hazards
18 Gained
19 Alerts
22 Diva

91

Across

4 Gambol
5 Errs
7 Patriot
10 Filch
11 Traitor
12 Riled
14 Strange
15 Piste
16 Algiers
20 Chary
21 Cayenne
22 Peel
23 Fedora

Down

1 Smart
2 Cocoa
3 Prairie
4 Gear
6 Sacked
8 Irately
9 Titanic
10 Forgery
13 Bishop
14 Started
17 Eager
18 Señor
19 Inca

92

Across

1 Blind
4 Dally
10 Summons
11 Doone
12 Extra
13 Ensnare
15 Tore
17 Greed
19 Abode
22 Date
25 Verbose
27 Strip
29 Rodeo
30 In doubt
31 Users
32 Ashen

Down

2 Lumet
3 Neonate
5 Andes
6 Leopard
7 Osier
8 Usher
9 Sever
14 Neat
16 Odds
18 Reredos
20 Besides
21 Overt
23 Aegis
24 Spate
26 Odour
28 Rouse

93

Across

5 Salvo
8 Latterly
9 Faint
10 Critical
11 Feral
14 Bed
16 Panama
17 Agrees
18 Yam
20 State
24 Bactrian
25 Twist
26 Ruminate
27 Byway

Down

1 Slick
2 Attic
3 Merit
4 Sleaze
6 Amateurs
7 Vintages
12 Castaway
13 Fantasia
14 Bay
15 Dam
19 Abacus
21 Stoic
22 Milan
23 Sneer

94

Across
1 Timon
4 Motion
9 Studies
10 Elver
11 Lady
12 Reptile
13 Top
14 Dodo
16 Ache
18 Cry
20 Lottery
21 Stoa
24 Dogma
25 Lanolin
26 Ranger
27 Gaped

Down
1 Tussle
2 Mound
3 Nail
5 Overplay
6 Inveigh
7 Nerved
8 Usurp
13 Tolerate
15 Octagon
17 Glider
18 Cycle
19 Warned
22 Tulip
23 Snag

95

Across
1 Neck
3 Terrines
9 Carve
10 Cover-up
11 Raw
13 Desperate
14 Attila
16 Lariat
18 Tasteless
20 Era
22 Elastic
23 Leave
25 Sidestep
26 Chat

Down
1 Nicer
2 Car
4 Excise
5 Riviera
6 Narrative
7 Sapient
8 Need
12 Withstand
14 Antlers
15 Laertes
17 Rescue
19 Sell
21 Agent
24 Ash

96

Across
7 Across
8 Sticks
10 Mansion
11 Trade
12 Sell
13 Score
17 Snoop
18 High
22 Newer
23 Entreat
24 Minute
25 Clumsy

Down
1 Palmist
2 Wrinkle
3 Astir
4 Stature
5 Scrap
6 Asked
9 Anecdotes
14 Untruth
15 Dilemma
16 Shut-eye
19 Enemy
20 Swank
21 Stalk

97

Across
1 New
3 Row
5 Seas
7 Isles
8 Ration
10 Hook
11 Question
13 Oregon
14 Edible
17 Reformer
19 Ooze
21 Visits
22 Roast
23 Thug
24 Tax
25 End

Down
1 Neighbours
2 Welcome
3 Risk
4 Warm-up
5 Set-aside
6 Aioli
9 Interested
12 Hoarding
15 Brocade
16 Jet set
18 Faith
20 Oryx

98

Across
1 Aries
4 Tourer
9 Crowbar
10 Gauge
11 Skye
12 Winsome
13 Pad
14 Howl
16 Sash
18 Opt
20 Titanic
21 Drip
24 Ombre
25 Article
26 Gyrate
27 Doyen

Down
1 Access
2 Ivory
3 Sobs
5 Organist
6 Raucous
7 Reeled
8 Crowd
13 Plangent
15 October
17 Strong
18 Ocean
19 Spleen
22 Rocky
23 Stud

99

Across
1 Abigail
5 Storm
8 Felon
9 Snowdon
10 Evil eye
11 Parts
12 Silent
14 Orient
17 Grunt
19 Brother
22 Entered
23 Tense
24 Stall
25 Streets

Down
1 Alfie
2 Ill-will
3 Annie
4 Listed
5 Stopper
6 Order
7 Mindset
12 Signets
13 Natural
15 Enhance
16 Abides
18 Ultra
20 Outer
21 Reels

100

Across
1 Extra
5 Curry
8 Color
9 Plait
10 Inception
11 Lei
12 Chain letter
15 Request stop
19 UFO
20 Soap opera
22 Neigh
23 Icing
24 Dryad
25 Eject

Down
1 Espalier
2 Tragic
3 Activate
4 Flacon
5 Crop
6 Relict
7 Yawn
13 Estrange
14 Ricochet
16 Quarry
17 Thesis
18 Pumice
20 Skid
21 Ovid

101

Across
1 Rough
4 Aeons
10 Richest
11 Alter
12 Larva
13 Retired
15 Damp
17 Steam
19 Eagle
22 Poem
25 Protest
27 Idler
29 Ratio
30 Embrace
31 Order
32 Sever

Down
2 Occur
3 Grenada
5 Exact
6 Natural
7 Grill
8 Storm
9 Crude
14 Epee
16 Amps
18 Trotter
20 Amiable
21 Spurn
23 Otter
24 Greed
26 Erode
28 Leave

102

Across
1 Hiker
4 Manned
9 Averted
10 Odium
11 Sulk
12 Glamour
13 Awe
14 Acid
16 Lair
18 Due
20 Unaware
21 Glut
24 Basic
25 Traffic
26 Deride
27 Nasty

Down
1 Hoarse
2 Kneel
3 Rite
5 Adorable
6 Nairobi
7 Demure
8 Adage
13 Advanced
15 Coarser
17 Curbed
18 Depth
19 Sticky
22 Lifts
23 Fawn

103

Across

1 Speck
4 Tater
10 Conquer
11 Pluto
12 Malta
13 Grandee
15 Dose
17 Aztec
19 Nehru
22 Hide
25 Hamster
27 Remix
29 Sieve
30 Needful
31 Birds
32 Straw

Down

2 Panel
3 Crusade
5 Alpha
6 Ecuador
7 Scamp
8 Dregs
9 Joker
14 Rend
16 Oche
18 Zambezi
20 Eeriest
21 Ghost
23 Irony
24 Exile
26 Tweed
28 Mafia

104

Across

5 Franc
8 Einstein
9 Judge
10 Adequate
11 Party
14 One
16 Stanza
17 Bylaws
18 Fob
20 Tweet
24 Additive
25 Swoop
26 Stickler
27 Pyrex

Down

1 Medal
2 Onset
3 Stout
4 Kitten
6 Reusable
7 Night-owl
12 Stowaway
13 Envelope
14 Oaf
15 Ebb
19 Oddity
21 Hitch
22 Villa
23 Merry

www.ingramcontent.com/pod-product-compliance
Ingram Content Group UK Ltd.
Pitfield, Milton Keynes, MK11 3LW, UK
UKHW040639280225
455688UK00002B/20